Denmark: An Archaeological Guide

Archaeological Guides

General Editor: GLYN DANIEL

Sicily Margaret Guido

Southern Greece Robert and Kathleen Cook

Denmark:
An Archaeological Guide

ELISABETH MUNKSGAARD

FABER AND FABER LIMITED
LONDON

First published in 1970
by Faber and Faber Limited
24 Russell Square, London, W.C.1
Printed in Great Britain
by Ebenezer Baylis and Son, Limited
The Trinity Press, Worcester, and London
All rights reserved

ISBN 0 571 09196 2

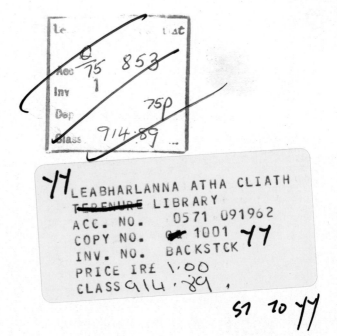
© *1970 by Elisabeth Munksgaard*

Contents

Tables

Illustrations

Preface

A Danish archaeologist cannot imagine that any Englishman in his senses would dream of buying this book and visiting Denmark, thereby exchanging the inclemency of his own climate for one which is—if possible—even worse. There are two winters in Denmark: a white and a green one, and the latter is by far the worse. Piercing winds and icy showers have in no time broken even the strongest spirits. But if you, to quote a famous Queen, 'pluck up your hearts and fear them not' you shall have your reward—no less than 23,000 prehistoric monuments await your inspection (the number covers the amount of monuments protected by the Ancient Monuments Act, but only a fraction of the original number: 78,000). From this amazing number it has of course been necessary to select the best and most characteristic of a given area.

A good map is of course indispensable to the archaeologically-minded traveller as prehistoric monuments have a deplorable habit of tucking themselves away in the most improbable and inaccessible corners even of our tiny, crowded country. I shall recommend the 1 cm maps in three volumes (scale 1 : 100,000) published by Geodætisk Institut (the Danish Ordnance Survey). If you would like to study a smaller area thoroughly there are excellent 4 cm maps (scale 1 : 25,000) on which the prehistoric monuments are marked with various signs. The only problem is that the 4 cm maps do not yet cover the whole country.

And now a few words of warning: most prehistoric monuments are found on private land, and no farmer will look benevolently at strangers tramping across his fields to inspect whatever monument is placed there. All Ancient Monuments are commended to the protection and care of visitors. If you enter a passage grave or a dolmen chamber do not leave litter about or cause any disorder, do not disturb the lie of the stones or try to remove the small stones from walls or roof as it may involve a danger of collapse.

The author has not pretended to plan any itineraries for the archaeologically-minded traveller. The country is divided into smaller areas (map, p. 21) and within each the monuments are listed alphabetically with a short description of how to get there and a description of the site. Each chapter (area) ends with a description of the principal museums and the towns within the area from which it will be most convenient to set out. But these are only meant as suggestions; Denmark is after all such a small country that you can travel from one end to the other in less than a day.

ELISABETH MUNKSGAARD

A Short Outline of Danish Prehistory

The first traces of human activity on Danish soil are from the arctic period of the postglacial age. Stray bands of reindeer hunters have left antler axes and flint arrow-heads, but only one settlement site is known so far, that of Bromme in Central Zealand dating from the Allerød period, the only palæolithic culture known from Denmark.

During the mesolithic period hunters and fishers settled on the banks of the numerous lakes which are now vast peat bogs. One of the oldest of these sites is Klosterlund in Central Jutland, about the age of the English site at Star Carr in Yorkshire, dating from the preboreal period. From the later, boreal period many sites are known such as the classic mesolithic dwelling places at Holmegaard, Mullerup, Sværdborg and Aamosen. These sites—all in Zealand—are centred on the banks of the prehistoric lakes whereas the contemporary sites in Jutland—the Gudenaa culture—are found on sandy soil near the river banks, especially along the rivers Gudenaa and Skernaa. As the land was raised much higher than now we do not know of any settlements on the sea coasts.

During the atlantic period a series of transgressions altered the land so that the level of land and sea was much like what it is now. Northern Jutland lay lower than now whereas the southern part of the country was raised higher. This is the period of the kitchen middens, the shell-mounds of the Ertebølle culture, accumulated by the hunters and fishers who lived near the coast and fed on oysters and sea shells and hunted the game of the oak-mixed forests which had by this time superseded the pine forests of the boreal period. The climate was warmer and more humid than now. From the Ertebølle period date our oldest visible monuments of prehistoric date, i.e. the shell-mounds which are found in the northern parts of the country on raised beaches above the present sea level. The most famous of these mounds is the Ertebølle kitchen-midden (Area 8, No. 7) which gave its name to the culture. In South Denmark most of the shell-mounds are now submerged.

The first farmers arrived in Denmark about 2700 B.C. They brought domesticated animals such as cattle, sheep and goats, and began to cultivate small strips of land where they grew barley and wheat. They made neat little clay pots of so-called funnel-beaker types. They buried their dead in simple trench graves, either flat graves or covered by low mounds. But gradually the 'megalithic religion' spread to these people and the stone-built dolmens began to appear. The oldest dolmen chamber is a simple rectangular chamber built of four uprights and one capstone, covered with earth and surrounded by a circle of peristaliths. The pretty dolmen chamber (deprived of its covering mound) which is more or less a Danish national symbol was never meant to be seen; it was covered by an earth mound. But what really mattered was the encircling ring of raised stones which marked the boundaries of a sacred area belonging to the dead.

The early neolithic dwelling sites and graves show that the first farmers spread rapidly over the country. Dolmens are found all over Denmark. There is hardly a parish which cannot boast of one.

During the middle neolithic period (also known as the passage grave period) the culture of the funnel-beaker people soared to its heights. Their exquisite flint work and beautiful pottery cannot fail to impress those who see it today. The farmers buried their dead in huge, stone-built chambers which stood unto eternity. Dolmen chambers were still built and still in use—the solid megaliths, the passage graves, began to appear during the earlier part of the period (about 2200 B.C.). The passage grave has a rectangular or oval chamber with a passage at right angles. The whole structure is covered with an earth mound bordered by small peristaliths, not nearly so imposing as those of the dolmens. During the later part of the period it seems that the idea of building passage graves was given up earlier in Jutland than in the islands. In Jutland the funnel-beaker people began to bury their dead in flat graves placed in long rows and covered by solid stone carpets, the so-called stone packing graves which are not known in the islands. Passage graves are known from most parts of the country except West Jutland and Vendsyssel and in many parts of the country they are placed within a stone's throw of each other. Population was dense where good and light soil was cultivated.

During this period stirring events took place in Jutland. A nation of warriors armed with battle-axes, equipped with odd earthenware vessels, and flint tools of poor workmanship, invaded Jutland from the south. They buried their dead under small, low barrows placed in groups in low-lying country. These warriors, who were more shepherds than farmers, spread rapidly over Jutland, and reinforced by related tribes from Holstein and North-west Germany, they at last settled in the islands as well. Their burial mounds in Jutland were often rebuilt and enlarged during the Bronze Age but there are still many to be seen as they were left by those who built them.

The rapid spread of the single-grave warriors can hardly have taken place without clashes with the indigenous population. We do not quite know what was the outcome of the more or less warlike contacts between the two nations, but during the late neolithic period it looks as if the single-grave culture had come victorious out of the battle.

The late neolithic period shows a rather uniform culture without marked differences from province to province. Excellent flint-work in daggers, arrow-heads, knives and sickles, coarse, unornamented pottery and a steady flow of imported bronze dominate the finds. The burial rites, however, change markedly from one district to another. In Jutland both single and common graves appear and both flat graves and barrows are in use. In North Jutland stone cists were much in use—both huge ones meant for several dead bodies and small ones for a single interment. The most characteristic burial type in Zealand was the stone cist built of slabs; this type of burial was also used both as single graves and as common graves. Dolmens and passage graves were no longer built, but those standing were still in use, several late neolithic burials come from megalithic tombs.

Dwelling sites are not very well known from this period. The most important one is from Gug in North Jutland where a house was found; the floor was littered with flint scraps and several finds of flint tools show that this house was inhabited by a flint 'smith'.

The many finds of imported bronze show that the metal-using era dawned at last. The Bronze Age began about 1500 B.C. and lasted for a thousand years. It has left to us such exquisite finds as the sun chariot, the woollen garments from oak coffins, the lurs—wind instruments of ear-splitting quality—and above all a manifestation of excellent workmanship in the casting of bronze and of a highly developed ornamental art. But above all the Bronze Age is the age of the burial mounds. By thousands and thousands they crown the hilltops or line the trackways to the sea—the all-important sea across which came ships laden with bronze and gold and to which merchants travelled with amber and fur to embark for enterprise and adventure. The Bronze Age chieftains placed the barrows on the most visible spots—'not to see but to be seen was their aim'.

Posterity was not kind to the burial monuments. Where they stood on fertile soil they were ruthlessly ploughed out, if they were not saved by superstition. But however hard posterity was there are still about ten thousand left—there is hardly a hilltop which is not crowned by an imposing Bronze Age barrow and we feel that they belong to our scenery which would look sad without them.

Most of the barrows were built during the early Bronze Age when inhumation was still the rule. The barrows cover a central grave, either a stone cist, a trunk coffin of oak or a coffin of planks. Towards the end of the early Bronze Age cremation was introduced and the grave shrank gradually until the burial urn dominated. The urns were almost always placed in the top or sides of existing barrows; only from the islands do we know of small barrows covering late Bronze Age urn burials.

Somehow the Bronze Age appears as a gigantic undertaker's establishment—so well do we know the dead, so little the living. Compared to the number of burials, dwelling sites, not to speak of houses, are almost unknown. It seems as if the Bronze Age people lived more like the single-grave warriors; they were more shepherds than farmers, and above all they were engaged in trade.

The rock engravings show their religion as do the many votive offerings of both weapons and female ornaments. The climate was warm and dry and the sun was worshipped as the great invigorator of life. The axe was worshipped as the warrior's important weapon and the ship is often found on the rock engravings. On board a ship the sun sailed across the sky and on board a ship the chieftains brought home wealth and luxury.

The Iron Age began about 500 B.C. with a deterioration of climate which must have had a remarkable influence on a primitive farming culture. The climate became cold and humid and the oak-mixed forest gradually gave way to that of the beech—in the Celtic Iron Age the typical Danish summer and the typical Danish woods were born.

With the Bronze Age the great barrow-building era was over. From South and West Jutland we know of cemeteries of small, low mounds covering urn burials—during this period the gravefield appears for the first time, to remain until the end of prehistory—but in other parts of the country flat graves covering urns or cremation patches are the rule. Thus the Celtic Iron Age has left no imposing grave monuments, but on the other hand such sites as prehistoric fields and houses, especially on the moors of Jutland. The most imposing site is undoubtedly the Borremose stronghold and village (Area 8, No. 3).

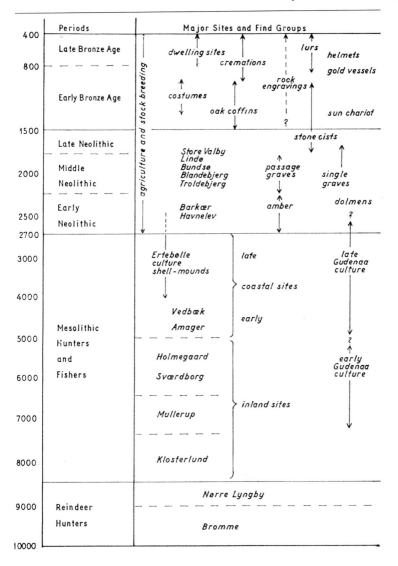

	Periods	Major Sites and Find Groups
400		
	Late Bronze Age	dwelling sites lurs helmets
800		cremations gold vessels
	Early Bronze Age	costumes rock engravings
		oak coffins sun chariot
1500		?
	Late Neolithic	stone cists
2000	Middle Neolithic	Store Valby, Lindø, Bundsø, Blandebjerg, Troldebjerg passage graves single graves
2500	Early Neolithic	Barkær, Havnelev amber dolmens ?
2700		
3000		Ertebølle culture shell-mounds late late Gudenaa culture
4000		coastal sites
5000	Mesolithic Hunters	Vedbæk, Amager early
6000	and Fishers	Holmegaard, Sværdborg ? early Gudenaa culture
7000		Mullerup inland sites
8000		Klosterlund
9000	Reindeer Hunters	Nørre Lyngby
10000		Bromme

(left vertical label: agriculture and stock breeding)

Table 1. Chronological table of the Stone and Bronze Ages

2

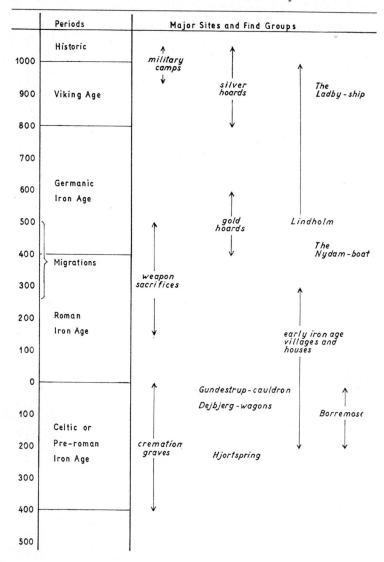

Table 2. Chronological table of the Iron Age

Finds of pottery from houses and graves show that the early Iron Age gradually developed from the Bronze Age. During the last centuries before the birth of Christ a strong influence appears from the Celtic culture with such remarkable finds as bronze cauldrons (sometimes used as urns), the justly famous Gundestrup cauldron, and the procession wagon from Dejbjerg. It also deserves mention that the oldest Danish ship, the Hjortspring boat from Als, dates from this period.

The Roman Iron Age (from about the time of the birth of Christ to A.D. 400) was a very rich period. We know of several villages, rich grave finds, and above all a wealth of Roman imports. Such quantities of Roman bronzes have been found that there can hardly have been a farm without at least one set of ladles and strainers and hardly a blue-eyed farmer's daughter without a string of fascinating glass beads round her neck. The prize goes to the Hoby burial treasure: two silver cups of exquisite Augustan workmanship, a jug, a situla, and a ladle, a bronze tray, and fine silver fibulæ.

Burial rites vary from one part of the country to another, which may show the first traces of a tribal community. The same division into distinct cultural areas is given by the pottery which is of great variety and excellent workmanship. Both cremation and inhumation graves are found, mostly as flat graves. Only North Jutland has visible grave monuments to offer: huge stone cists built of boulders, almost megalithic to look at.

The Germanic Iron Age (about 400–800) is poor in grave finds and village sites, but on this modest background the huge wealth of the gold hoards glimmers with a fascinating light. This is the age of the great, mythical heroes and also of heavy fights the spoils of which are found in sacred lakes and bogs: swords, arrows and spears, horses and mail shirts were sacrificed to the gods after the battles. Such a wealth of weapons is found in these sacred places that the lakes must have been used for several sacrifices throughout the late Roman and Germanic periods.

The Viking Age has left such imposing monuments as the royal mounds at Jelling (Area 4, No. 8), the military camps at Trelleborg (Area 18, No. 36) and Fyrkat (Area 7, No. 7), the Ladby ship burial (Area 12, No. 9)—our only ship burial; it seems as if this custom was more Swedish and Norwegian than Danish—and above all the burial ground and town at Lindholm near Aalborg (Area 11, No. 19), not to forget the innumerable rune-stones commemorating the dead.

Many burials are richly furnished with weapons, smiths' tools or female ornaments such as trilobate and tortoise-shaped brooches and glass beads; even remains of brocade and richly embroidered garments have been found—the Viking chieftain was a chieftain indeed. Rich silver hoards are abundant during the Viking period, showing partly the wealth of the population and partly that wars and raids were everyday occurrences.

1. Runic Alphabet of the Viking period

On the threshold of history came the conversion to Christianity about the end of the tenth century; it is commemorated on the larger Jelling stone on which Harold Bluetooth is called 'he who won all Denmark and Norway and christened the Danes'. Now, a thousand years later, we can see that Harold did his best, but that a whole nation does not give up its Old Gods at a royal command. Christianity came gradually and a hundred years after king Harold 600 village churches had been built. But paganism never died quite away—there are still so many prehistoric burial mounds full of trolls and dwarfs and so many peat bogs where hobgoblins lead people astray and the elves dance at night, their soft laughter mocking the church bells.

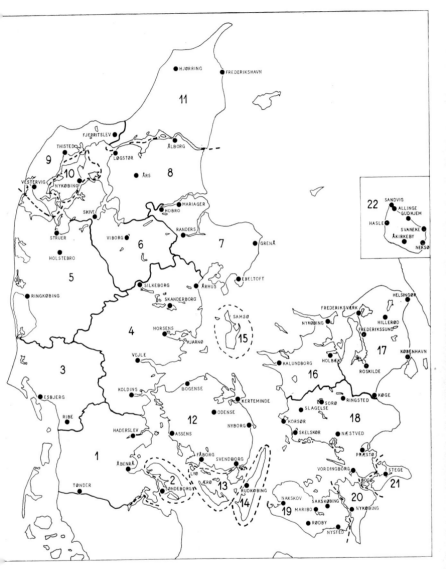

2. Denmark: Areas and principal towns

JUTLAND

Area 1. South Jutland

1: Birkelev: 5 km north-east of Skærbæk on the road between the villages Aved and Normsted is a stretch of moorland with thirty-one small barrows from the Celtic Iron Age.

2: Brøndlund: Between Gram and Toftlund is a large Bronze Age barrow, the last of a group of about thirty barrows placed along the banks of the small stream Gelså.

3: Brøns: 600 m west of the mill at Brøns village is a small group of Bronze Age barrows. 1 km to the east is another group of sixteen barrows.

4: Brøstrup: Near Rødding. A group of imposing Bronze Age barrows on a hill-top north of the village.

5: Flovt: South of the road Haderslev-Årøsund is a dolmen with a large capstone; the earth mound is not preserved.

6: Frøslev: South-west of the village near the German frontier are several barrows of imposing size (up to 4 m in height).

7: Gasse høje: A few km east of Skærbæk on the Skærbæk-Arild road near the North Sea coast is a group of twenty-seven barrows placed on a low hill.

8: Gram: In the wood east of Gram Castle park is a group of six barrows. West of Gram church is another group of five barrows.

9: Gråsten: In the woods west and north of Gråsten are ten long dolmens and twenty Bronze Age barrows. Most noteworthy are four long dolmens and two barrows in Gråsten Deer Park.

10: Harreby: Halfway along the road from Ribe to Rødding (about 10 km from Ribe) on a hill-top 200 m west of the road is a small Neolithic cemetery (the area is protected by the Ancient Monuments Act) with three dolmens and one stone cist; other graves within the area are flat graves. This Neolithic cementery with its collection of dolmens, cists and flat graves is the only one of its kind in Denmark. The graves have been excavated and the finds are in the Haderslev County Museum.

11: Hennekesdam: 2 km south-west of Jels is a big Bronze Age barrow more than 4 m high; it contained an oak coffin and remnants of woollen garments. The find is in the Haderslev County Museum.

12: Hjerpsted: On the North Sea coast between the villages Hjerpsted and Kolby is a group of barrows, originally numbering twenty-seven, but not all of them are preserved. Another group of twenty-two barrows is situated only 2 km south of Hjerpsted near Albæk farm.

13: The Hærulf rune-stone: On the west side of the ancient road through Jutland, Hærvejen (the Army Road, see Area 4, No. 7), between Hovslund and the ancient ford Immervad, is a rune-stone bearing the inscription Hairulfr (a man's name) dating from about A.D. 900. Opposite the rune-stone is a barrow, Strangelshøj, with a bauta stone.

14: Jels: A barrow is to be seen just south of the village beside the road to Oksenvad, the last one of a group of twenty barrows. On the road from Jels to Vamdrup are three little lakes. On the east bank of the Midtsø is an earthen wall in the form of a half circle, with a ditch. The date is uncertain but it is either late Viking or early Middle Ages. Inside the area framed by the wall is a dolmen chamber which has been moved from Jels and reconstructed here.

15: Kelstrup skov: South of the road A8 from Kruså to Sønderborg, near the coast of Flensborg Fjord, is a small wood with an imposing 40 m long dolmen with two burial chambers. Further south, in the Hønsnap wood, are six long and one round dolmen, and four barrows.

16: Kelstrupstrand: 10 km south-east of Haderslev, along the coast, are eleven barrows and at Hejsager strand are seven barrows in a small wood facing the coast.

Plate I. Late Neolithic stone cist, 'Myrpold', near Aabenraa (Area I, No. 19)

17: Kobbelskov: On the Broagerland peninsula south-east of Gråsten, about 10 km south-east of Broager is a small wood called Kobbelskov with about ten dolmens and ten barrows. Two long dolmens measure 13 and 20 m respectively and each has two burial chambers.

18: Lokeshøje: East of Københoved on the road from Vejen to Skodborg. Four barrows on a hill-top. About sixty barrows are scattered on the hills and on the plain between the hills and the river Kongeåen.

19: Myrpold: A stone cist in a field near the coast south-east of Løjt Skovby, not far from Åbenrå. The cist contained clay vessels and axes from the battle-axe culture; the finds are in Århus Prehistoric Museum.

20: Over Jerstal: West of the road from Vojens to Over Jerstal about 2 km north of Over Jerstal is a small enclosed area with three barrows, two of which cover passage graves to which access is possible.

21: Skibelundbjerg: 5 km east of Gram on a hill west of Skibelund are two barrows belonging to a large group which reached from Vojens to Nustrup and Gram. In Nustrup plantation, west of the road from Rødding to Nustrup, are the last remains of a group which stretched from Nustrup to Vrå. Fladhøj (the flat barrow) is situated 800 m north of Skibelundbjerg; its diameter is about 60 m and it once covered a passage grave.

22: Slaghøj: About 4 km north-west of Rødding near Skærbæk mill is a long dolmen and several barrows. A lane leads to the field along the east side of Skærbæk mill pond.

23: Tamdruphøj: On the south side of Haderslev Fjord north of the road from Haderslev to Hajstrup is a most impressive barrow, 42 m in diameter and not less than 9 m in height. The barrow, which is one of the largest in Denmark, commands a splendid view of Lillebælt and the surrounding countryside.

24: Toppehøj: 5 km north of Tinglev and just south of Bolderslev is a group of five barrows, all that remains of the original eighteen. Toppehøj is the northernmost of the group; this barrow contained an Early Bronze Age burial with textiles and weapons which is now in the National Museum.

25: Vedsted: About 10 km south-west of Haderslev on the road to Over Jerstal is an area about 2 × 1.5 km, between Vedsted and Abkær, scattered with about a hundred barrows. At Vedsted is a group of six barrows, on the road from Vedsted is a long dolmen, where the road to Abkær crosses the road from Vedsted is a long dolmen (45 m long) with one rectangular chamber in which was found a collared flask now in Haderslev County Museum. At Holmshus is a large barrow covering a passage grave (the entrance is a reconstruction) and west of this are three long dolmens two of which are 92 and 115 m in length. One of the easternmost barrows in the area is Pothøj, placed on a hill-top of 80 m height.

26: Vongshøj: About 4 km north-west of Løgumkloster and west of the road to Arild. The barrow is the largest one in a group of about fifty. In the oak shrubs to the north are five barrows.

The principal museum of the area is Haderslev County Museum (Åstrupvej, Haderslev) which is the archaeological museum of North

Slesvig. The museum is open daily from 10–12 a.m. and from 2–5 p.m. except Thursdays.

Abenrå Museum (Main Street, Abenrå) has a good archaeological collection. The museum is open from 10–12 a.m. and 2–5 p.m. except Mondays.

Haderslev is well situated for visits to the sites Nos. 2, 4, 5, 8, 11, 14, 16, 18, 20, 22, 23 and 25 (No. 8 can equally well be approached from Ribe). The coach station is at Nørregade. Tourist information at Nørregade 41. Hotels: Harmonien, Gåskærgade 19; Höppners Hotel, Nørregade 22; Motel Haderslev, Damparken and Missionshotellet, Jomfrustien 22.

Ribe is a good starting point for the Nos. 1, 3, 7, 10 and 21 (21 can just as well be approached from Haderslev). About Ribe, see area 3, South West Justland, page 36.

Åbenrå is well situated for visits to the sites Nos. 9, 13, 15, 17, 19 and 24 (Nos. 15 and 17 can just as well be approached from Sønderborg see Area 2, Als, page 29). Coaches run to all parts of South Jutland. The coach station is at H.P. Hansensgade 48. The Tourist Information office is at H.P. Hansensgade 5. Hotels: Hoide Hus; Grand Hotel H.P. Hansensgade 10; Folkehjem, Nørre Chausse 7; and Danmark, Nørreport 13.

Tønder is well situated for visits to Nos. 12 and 26. The coach station is at the Østbanegård. The Tourist Information office is at Skibbroen 13. Hotels: Tønderhus, Jomfrustien; Missionshoteller, Storegade 9; and Hagge's Hotel, Vestergade 80.

Area 2. Als

1: Blommenskobbel: A small wood on the east coast a few km north of A8 to Mommark. In the northern part is a remarkable group of megalithic monuments—two long dolmens and two round dolmens; a little further south is a third round dolmen and further west near the northern limit of the wood is a long dolmen.

2: Brandsbøl wood: A few km south of Nordborg. Some 400 m east of the wood on the north side of the road is a long dolmen, 60 m long; west of the hedge that runs across the dolmen is a dolmen chamber, in which have been found an amber bead, a flint chisel and some potsherds. The finds are in Sønderborg Museum. South of the road are two long dolmens of which the eastern one contains a small passage grave. In the south-east corner of the wood are two long dolmens.

3: Brovold: Near Augustenborg, situated between the main road and the road to Miang. Brovold is a Viking and early mediaeval town protected by an earthen wall which can still be seen east of the main road. Excavations carried out in the 1930's showed traces of small, square huts. Finds from Brovold are in Sønderborg Museum.

4: Havnbjerg (or Hagenbjerg): 3 km east of Nordborg. In the small wood about 2 km north of the village is a long dolmen, 35 m long, situated in the southern part of the wood near the road. The dolmen contained a long, rectangular cist, with a single burial which is now in Sønderborg Museum.

At Havnbjerg Church is a stone with cup-marks, placed in the wall surrounding the cemetery.

5: Lambjerg Indtægt: A small wood 5 km east of Sønderborg. North of the main road near the western limit of the wood is a barrow 4 m high and opposite this (at the other side of the road) is a megalithic chamber, 3.60 m long and built of nine stones. In the wood are about thirty more barrows and two long dolmens near the western limit not far from the road.

6: Nørreskov: On the east coast of Als between Hellevad and Klingbjerg, in the western part of the wood, near Nygård, is a pretty round dolmen, and south of Nygård are two small long dolmens. Further south on the lane from Østerholm to Taksensand on the coast are three long dolmens; 200 m to the north of these monuments is the round dolmen Gamle Troldhøj. Just north of Frydendal inn near Hellevad are a round and a long dolmen, and just east of the wood and on the other side of the road are three barrows. On the beach about 400 m from the lighthouse is a stone with cup-marks.

7: Oleskobbel: A small wood on the east coast south of Nørreskoven. On the coast, about 200 m from the wood, are two dolmens together encircled by the same ring of peristaliths, ninety-six in all. The two dolmens are each 30 m long and about 14 m across. Each dolmen has a chamber without capstones.

8: Sønderskov: Just east of Sønderborg. One of the nicest areas of prehistoric monuments on Als. In the northern part of the wood are several large barrows up to 4 m in height, in the central part several smaller ones. On both sides of the main road leading through the wood are about ten barrows varying in height from 1 to 2 m.

The principal museum is at Sønderborg Castle. The museum has a good local prehistoric collection. Although it is the principal historical museum of South Jutland with special regard to the 1848–51 and 1864 wars it has a small prehistoric collection.

The museum is open during the summer season from 10 a.m.–6 p.m. and during the winter season from 1–4 p.m.

Sønderborg is the county town and the 'metropolis' of Als. Several good hotels are at the traveller's disposal such as Alssund, Alhambra Dybbølgade 2; Missionshotellet Ansgar, Nørrebro 2; Rådhushotellet Hildebrand Rådhustorvet 6; and Strand, Strandvej 1.

The Tourist Information office is at Kirketorvet.

Smaller hotels are to be found at Nordborg and Augustenborg and at the seaside is the Baltic Hotel at Hørup Hav about 10 km east of Sønderborg.

Coaches run from Sønderborg to Nordborg—Holm, to Hundslev—Stevning—Nordborg, to Fynshav—Skovby, and to Fynshav—Kegnæs.

Area 3. South-West Jutland

1: Askov: 2 km from Vejen south of A1 is a stone with cup-marks, placed at the gates leading to Askov højskole. The stone is said to come from a ploughed-down barrow near Maltbæk old vicarage.

2: Borre: About 1 km north-east of Ål church on the road from Varde to Oksbøl are two groups of Bronze Age barrows.

3: Bramminge: 1 km west of the town on A11 is Stejlgård farm on the northern side of the road; in its fields stand three Bronze Age barrows—all that are left of a group of about ten. Further north-west of Bramminge along A11 is Korskroen (the Crossroad Inn), 1 km north of the inn is the large barrow called 'Arnhøj'.

4: Esbjerg: Confess, oh traveller, have you ever seen anything of Esbjerg but the Parkeston Quay and the railway station? But there is much to be seen—even several prehistoric monuments in the heart of the town. Two barrows from the Battle-Axe Culture can be seen behind the houses Nos. 72 and 78, Storegade, a third is near the school at No. 9 Haraldsgade, and a fourth is in a (private!) garden at No. 123, Grundtvigs alle. On the outskirts of the town (along A1) is Jerne church with a barrow in the south-west corner of the cemetery. East of Jerne rectory (south of A1) is Skibhøj, a long barrow which covered two Neolithic passage graves originally covered by separate mounds which were joined into one during the Bronze Age.

5: Frisvad: 4 km along A11 north of Varde is Frisvad where several barrows, probably from the Battle-Axe Culture are to be seen in the moors and the plantations surrounding the village. Some of the barrows are more than 3 m in height; they probably date from the Bronze Age.

6: Grimstrup krat (= shrubs): North of A1 about 15 km east of Esbjerg, between Korskroen (cf. No. 3) and Grimstrup is the wood

Grimstrup krat. In the south-western part is a group of five barrows, and a few hundred metres north of this group in the western part of the wood are several Iron Age fields to be seen framed by low earthen walls (lynchets). In the north-eastern part of the wood not far from the Omme to Rovst road is a dyke 200 m long—Kampdiget—with an eastward facing ditch. The date of this dyke has not been determined.

7: Henne: From Varde to Ovtrup and west to Henne kirkeby. Between Blåbjerg and Henne is a group of about ten large barrows, among which is a long barrow, all placed on a long, low hill which commands beautiful views of the sand dunes and the North Sea.

8: Horne: About 10 km north of Varde along A11, turn right (east) at the 50 km stone to Horne, where south of the church a rune-stone is placed, it was found in the cemetery wall in the seventeenth century. Only a fragment is now left which bears the inscription, 'Tue, Ravn's scion made Th....s (or: this) burial mound'. (See also No. 11.)

9: Langsig: About 12 km north of Varde along A11, turn west to Kvong and Lydum; halfway between these villages and about 2 km north-west of Lunde is Langsig, where on a stretch of moorland six barrows from the Battle-Axe Culture still remain, the remnants of an original twenty-five. In between these is a vast stretch of moorland with several prehistoric monuments. In the south-western part is a group of five smaller barrows, probably from the Battle-Axe Culture; in the central part of the moor are seven barrows the larger of which may be of Bronze Age date.

10: Lindknud: Between Lindknud and Vittrup, south of the wood, is a long dolmen with a fine chamber. A few kilometres to the west is the Klelund plantation with a very fine long dolmen and a round dolmen with a large chamber. Just south of Klelund village is a long dolmen not less than 117 m long.

11: Læborg: A few km north of Vejen (on A1) is Læborg parish church with a rune-stone placed in the cemetery. The stone was found in the seventeenth century in a field about 500 m north of the church. The inscription runs: 'Tue, Ravns scion, made these runes to Tyre, his queen'. Thor's hammer is engraved in the stone. The inscription is closely related to the Horne inscription (No. 8) and the Bække stone (Area 4, No. 1).

Plate 2. The passage grave at Mejls (Area 3, No. 13) photographed during the excavation in 1901

12: Marebæk plantation: About 10 km from Varde to Hostrup and then west to the plantation facing Ho bay. In this plantation are several Iron Age fields (lynchets) to be seen; especially in the part east of the road from Sjælborg to Tarphage. (Cf. also No. 16.)

13: Mejls: About 5 km north of Varde along A11, turn east to Mejls at the 55 km stone. One of the very few passage graves in West Jutland. The earthen mound was removed during the excavation in 1901, the chamber has seven uprights and two capstones. Inside the peristaliths is a broad 'collar' of small stones. The finds from Mejls are in the National Museum.

14: Nørholm moor: About 10 km from Varde on the Varde–Grindsted –Vejle road is Nørholm Manor, south of which is a vast stretch of moorland with several prehistoric monuments. In the south-western part is a group of five small barrows, probably from the Battle-Axe Culture; in the central part of the moor are seven barrows the larger of which may be of Bronze Age date.

15: Nørreskoven: Esbjerg golf course north of the town, near Gjesing plantation. On the golf course several Iron Age fields can be seen.

16: Sjælborg: (cf. No. 12) Follow the road sign through Sjælborg plantation past Baunehøj to the Iron Age houses. The contours of these houses from the Early Iron Age are preserved after excavation. The houses are of the ordinary Early Iron Age type, rectangular, the western half being the living-room and the eastern half the cow-byre. Characteristic of the South-West Jutland houses is the cobbled cow-byre, known only in the vicinity of Esbjerg. The finds from the Sjælborg houses are in Esbjerg Museum.

17: Skast: 10 km from Esbjerg along A1, north-west of Nørre Skast church is an imposing barrow, Baunehøj. Some 100 m to the south is an early dolmen with a square chamber built of four uprights and a large capstone.

18: Skonager: 5 km east of Varde on the Varde–Øse road is Skonager moor, on the western part of which several Iron Age fields are preserved. Three low barrows probably date from the Battle-Axe Culture.

19: Sønder Boel: 5 km east of Bramminge on the road from Bramminge to Holsted station, and 2 km to the south, is a small passage grave only 3 m long. The chamber is built with eight uprights and two capstones.

20: Tobøl: On the Ribe–Holsted road, about 15 km from Ribe. Near Tobøl are six large barrows, among which is 'Storhøj'. A few km to the west, at Plovstrup, are two barrows, Frishøj and Sortehøj.

21: Vorbasse: On the Grindsted–Lunderskov road, nor far from Lindknud (No. 10). South of the town, west of the road to Bække, is a long dolmen 63 m long, with three burial chambers. 1.5 km north-east of Vorbasse is the hill Store Baun, with seven barrows dating from the Battle-Axe Culture. West of the same road near Nørre Søgård plantation is a long dolmen with four burial chambers.

The principal museums are at Ribe and Esbjerg. Ribe museum, 'The Antiquarian Collections', is at Hans Tavsens house by the Cathedral. The collection comprises many good finds from Ribe county, especially of the Battle-Axe Culture and Bronze Age. The museum is open daily from 10–12 a.m. and 2–4 p.m. Fridays also 7–8 p.m.

Esbjerg museum, Finsensgade 1, has a good collection of objects from the Battle-Axe Culture and large, excellent collections of Early Iron Age pottery from the many house-sites excavated by the museum in the vicinity of Esbjerg. The museum is open weekdays, except Mondays, from 2–5 p.m., Sundays also from 10–12 a.m. During the winter season only Tuesdays, Saturdays and Sundays.

There are smaller, local museums also at Varde, Grindsted and Ølgod.

Esbjerg should make a good starting point for the monuments Nos. 3, 4, 6, 15–17 and 19. The coach station is at Jernbanegade and the Tourist Office at Torvet 21.

Choice of Hotels: Britannia, Torvet; Bangs Hotel, Torvet; Central Hotel, Torvet; Hotel Esbjerg, Skolegade 29; Paladshotellet, Skolegade 14; Hotels Spangsberg, Havnegade 75; two Missionshoteller, Skolegade 36 and 45; Hafnia, Skolegade 20.

Varde is an equally good starting point for the sites Nos. 2, 5, 7–9, 12–14, 16 and 18. Coaches start from Rådhusstræde, the Tourist Office is at Skansen 4.

Hotels: Hotel Varde, Storegade 3; Platzborg, Hjertingvej 2; Centralhotellet, Torvet; Dania, Storegade 19.

Ribe is a good starting point for No. 20 and for the Bramminge sites (listed above under Esbjerg). It is also a charming town. Coaches start from Dagmarsgade and the Tourist Office is at Storegade 10.

Hotels: Klubben, Skolegade; Dagmar, Torvet; Munken, Sct. Catarinæ Plads.

Vejen is well situated for the sites Nos. 1, 10, 11 and 21. Coaches from Esbjerg, Haderslev and Vejle. Trains from Fredericia and Esbjerg. Hotels: Hansens Hotel, Jernbanepladsen and Vejen Gæstgivergård.

Area 4. East Jutland

1: Bække: 1 km north of the Vejle–Ribe road is a ship-formed burial dating from the Viking period with a rune-stone placed as the stern and two Bronze Age barrows, the Klebæk barrows. The 'ship' is 45 m long, 6.5 m broad and the stones up to 2 m in height—the highest stones are placed nearest to the stern and stem of the ship. Of the original sixty stones only nine are preserved. The ship contained an empty, plundered burial. The inscription on the rune-stone says: 'Revne and Tobbe made this memorial to their mother Vibrog'.

Plate 3. Air photograph of the Bronze Age barrows and the ship-formed burial at Bække (Area 4, No. 1) after excavation and restoration in 1958

At Bække church is a rune-stone, the original place of which is unknown. The inscription says: 'Tue, Ravn's scion, and Funden and Gnyble, those three made Tyra's burial mound'. It is uncertain whether this inscription has any bearing on the Jelling monument (see No. 8), it is, however, closely related to the Læborg (Area 3, No. 11) and Horne stones (Area 3, No. 8).

2: Deelhøj, near Åstrup. From Horsens to Glud and then about 5 km south to Åstrup. Deelhøj is a pretty little passage grave with a circular chamber about 3 m in diameter, 1.70 m high and with a 4 m long passage leading to the chamber. The passage grave has yielded potsherds of Middle Neolithic date.

3: 'Gammelmand' (i.e. 'The old man') or Skanhøj. A10 out of Horsens and then left along the Østbirk road, turn left at Julianelyst Manor and then south to Skanhede. 'Gammelmand' is a fine round dolmen with a rectangular chamber of three uprights, one capstone, and a lintel, surrounded by a mound.

4: Grønhøj, in Bygholm park, just west of Horsens on the south bank of the lake. The passage grave Grønhøj is 3 m high and 25 m in diameter. The chamber measures 3.5 × 2.7 m and is built of seven uprights and two capstones; the passage is 4 m long. Grønhøj was excavated in 1940 and yielded rich finds of Middle Neolithic pottery, which are in Horsens Museum.

5: Gylling church: 15 km south of Odder. A rune-stone which was found in 1836 is now placed in the church. The rather worn inscription cannot be read in detail but has been deciphered as: 'Toke, Troels's son, made this stone to . . . good and Risbiik his brother'.

6: Hjarnø is a tiny little island at the south side of Horsens Fjord. Take the road from Horsens to Glud and from Glud to Snaptun where a ferry will take you to Hjarnø. On the south-eastern part of the island is a group of small ship-formed burials probably from the Viking period. Ten ships are more or less preserved, all that are left of a group of twenty.

7: Hærvejen: ('The Army Road'). The ancient road through Jutland from Viborg to Slesvig. From Viborg to Hundshoved it is buried under the asphalt of A3, but from Hundshoved to Randbøl is a beautiful stretch of fairly undisturbed scenery. South of Hovtrup is a low earthen dyke 'Margrethediget', the age of which is uncertain. The road passes Øster Nykirke, Kollemorten and Givskud, and from Mølvang it is only 3 km to Jelling (see No. 8); from Mølvang the road passes Trolderup and Nørup to Randbøl; here many Bronze Age barrows can be seen. North of Bække the road joins the Vejle–Ribe road. Near the crossroads at Kragelund a short stretch of the road is protected by the Ancient Monuments Act.

The ancient road, or rather trackway, is not built for cars. Best of all is, of course, to ride or walk—'but tread humbly in the worn tracks along which marched a thousand years of Danish history' (Hugo Mathiessen: *Hærvejen*).

8: Jelling: 12 km from Vejle along A18. The royal site of the Viking kings Gorm the Old and Harald Bluetooth. The two magnificent barrows just north and south of the church are the largest in Denmark and our oldest royal burials. Popular tradition dating back to the thirteenth century calls the northern mound 'Gorms høj' and the southern 'Tyres høj'. The northern barrow was excavated in the 1820's and was found to conceal a square chamber built of solid timber. The southern mound was excavated in the 1940's; it contained no burial. The monuments also include the two rune-stones in the cemetery and the rather enigmatic fifty bauta stones which may be the last remnants of a gigantic ship-formed monument.

The smaller rune-stone bears the inscription: 'Gorm king made these memorials to Tyre his queen, the mender of Denmark'. Whether the expression 'mender of Denmark' refers to Gorm or Tyre is uncertain. The larger rune-stone bears the inscription: 'King Harald made these memorials to Gorm, his father, and Tyre, his mother, the Harald who won all Denmark and Norway and christened the Danes'. To underline the conversion to Christianity the crucified Christ is seen on one side of the stone (the oldest Danish representation of Christ); on the other is a truly magnificent lion depicted in a style which without doubt reveals its maker to be of North English origin. The events mentioned on this fantastic stone took place about 980–90.

There were only a few finds from the Jelling excavations, as the burial chamber had been plundered. Most interesting is a small silver cup, which with the rest of the finds is in the National Museum.

9: **Lejrskov:** A group of eight barrows—originally the group consisted of about thirty. The remains of the others can still be seen as ploughed-down contours in the fields. Take A1 out of Kolding to the west, the group of barrows are placed on either side of a disused stretch of road north of A1 between the 11 and 13 km stones. Several of the barrows were excavated in the 1840's, the finds were Late Bronze Age urn burials and swords and knives from the Early Bronze Age.

10: **Palsgård skov** and the surrounding countryside. Beautiful scenery and many prehistoric monuments are to be found in the triangle between Nørre Snede (on the Horsens–Ejstrup road), Palsgård skov and Bryrup. The road through Palsgård skov to Vrads passes a group of five barrows, Ravnehøje; the south-eastern road to Boest leads to the five Godthåb barrows and further south-east to eight barrows in Boest shrubs. The smaller barrows probably date from the Battle-Axe Culture and the larger ones from the Bronze Age. Back to the Bryrup road, which passes Klovenhøj, and from Bryrup to Vrads where five small barrows are found just south of Vrads railway station. The road from Vrads through Grane plantation to Torup lake leads past a group of seven barrows.

11: **Randbøl:** (cf. also No. 7) Just south of the Vejle–Grindsted–Varde road, 20 km west of Varde. 'King Ran's barrow' is a flat-topped mound in Randbøl cemetery. Flat-topped mounds when excavated are almost always discovered to date from the late Roman Iron Age (cf. Vorbjerg No. 16). The Randbøl rune-stone is the only known rune-stone which is found in connection with a burial (the grave underneath the stone yielded, unfortunately, no finds), but the stone dates from the Viking Age and belongs to the considerable number of rune-stones found in the vicinity of the ancient 'Army Road'. The inscription reads: 'Bryden [i.e. a kind of mediaeval estate agent] Tue made this stone to his wife. These runes for Thorgun will live long'.

12: **Sjelle rune-stone:** From Århus to Framlev (by A15), then north-wards to Borum, then west to Sjelle. The rune-stone is now placed in the church. The stone is decorated with a mask which is known also from some other rune-stones. The rather worn text (the stone was once placed in the floor) reads, 'Frøsten made this stone to his "lagdsmand" Gyrd, Sigvald's brother, Tvegge's [?] . . . on . . . ed'.

13: Sønder Vissing rune-stones: About 25 km from Horsens on the Horsens–Silkeborg road to Brædstrup; just north of Brædstrup take the second turn to the right to Sdr. Vissing. Two rune-stones are kept in the church, the inscription on the larger one reads, 'Tove, Mistivi's daughter, wife of Harald the Good, Gorm's son, made these memorials to her mother'. Harald the Good may be Harald Bluetooth (but we do not know this 'nickname' or the name of his queen). The Slav king Mistivi is known from history, he sacked Hamburg in 983. The smaller stone has the inscription, 'Toke made these memorials to his father Ebbe, a wise man'.

14: Taps church: 12 km south of Kolding, just west of A10. There is a rock engraving of Bronze Age date just inside the main entrance. The engraving consists of three wheels, the popular symbol of Bronze Age sun worship.

15: Vinding: 4 km west of Bryrup (cf. No. 10) and 1 km north of Vinding village. A group originally consisting of eight barrows of which six are intact. The site commands a beautiful view of the surrounding hilly countryside. About 5 km west of the Vinding–Velling road are two long barrows which probably date from the Bronze Age.

16: Vorbjerg bakke: Between the Horsens–Silkeborg and the Horsens–Vorvadbro roads from Nim to Østbirk is an area rich in beautiful scenery and many prehistoric monuments. Eight large barrows on the top of Borbjerg hill are more or less flat-topped which seems to indicate an Iron Age date (cf. Randbøl, No. 11). One of these barrows contained an urn burial from the Late Roman Iron Age. South of this group is another of seven barrows among which is a long barrow. Further south, about 1 km north of Nim, is a group of eight barrows and cairns.

17: Ørum å: About 10 km east of Vejle, by A10 to Bredal, and from there to Engum and Daugård. East of Daugård in the wood on the west bank of Ørum å is one of the very few long dolmens of East Jutland. The dolmen is about 30 m long and has one chamber covered with three capstones, one of which is covered with cup-marks. The chamber was excavated in the 1930's and found to be plundered. The only finds were two flint axes and a chisel.

There are many museums in this district. The principal museum is Århus Prehistoric Museum at Moesgård (a former manor 10 km south of Århus). Among the objects there are the Grauballe peat-bog human sacrifice, the large weapon sacrifice from Illerup (Roman Iron Age) and the finds from Tustrup (see Area 7, No. 22).

Vejle Museum, Flegborg 16 has a good Stone Age collection and material from prehistoric iron smelting. Open daily from 10 a.m.–5 p.m. Sundays and Wednesdays free admission from 2–4 p.m.

Horsens Museum, Sundvej 1. The finds from Grønhøj and the Neolithic amber and copper treasure from Årupgård are specially noteworthy. Open 2–4 p.m. except Mondays; Sundays 10–12 a.m. and 2–4 p.m.

Silkeborg Museum: Prehistoric collections from the vicinity of the town, and also the head of the famous Tollund man, a human sacrifice from the Roman Iron Age. Open May to November 10–12 a.m. and 2.30–4.30 p.m.; during the winter season only Sundays, Wednesdays and Saturdays from 10–12 a.m. and 2–4 p.m.

Kolding Museum has a very good prehistoric collection. Open May to September from 9 a.m. to 6 p.m., April and October 10 a.m. to 4 p.m., November to March from 10 a.m. to 3 p.m.

Odder Museum, Møllevej 5, has a good local collection open weekdays 2–4 p.m., Sundays 10–12 a.m. and 3–6 p.m.

Gudenå Museum at Rye Bro has a large collection from the mesolithic sites which abound in the district—the Gudenå Culture. Open 9 a.m.–5 p.m. during the holiday season.

Århus is a good starting point for the sites Nos. 10 and 12 (No. 10 can also be approached from Silkeborg). The coach station is at Amtmandstoften near the harbour; the Tourist Information Office is at the Town Hall (the tower entrance). Some Hotels: Regina, Sønderalle 9; Ritz, Banegårdspladsen 12; Royal, Store Torv 4; Missions-hotellet Ansgar, Banegårdspladsen 14.

Odder should make a good starting point for site No. 5. Hotel: Centralhotellet, Rosensgade 18.

Silkeborg is well situated for the sites Nos. 7, 10, 13, 15 and 16 (13, 15 and 16 are just as easily reached from Horsens). Silkeborg is a pretty little town in the heart of Jutland surrounded by majestic hills and lovely lakes. A dense network of coach routes covers the neighbourhood. The Tourist Information Office is at Østergade 8. Hotels: Dania, Torvet; Missionshotellet at Drewsensvej 30 and Hostrupsgade 39.

Vejle is a good starting point for the sites Nos. 8, 11 and 17. Coaches run to most parts of Jutland. Tourist Information is at Dæmningen 19. Hotels: Australia, Grand, Orla Lehmannsgade 1; Caleb, Dæmningen 20.

Kolding for sites Nos. 1, 9 and 14. Excellent coach and train connections. Tourist Information Office at Helligkorsgade 18. Hotels: Kolding, Axeltorv 5; Saxildhus, Jernbanegade 39 (cuisine speciality: Swedish smørgåsbord and excellent pastries and cakes); Slotshoteilet, Jernbanegade 24. The coach station is at Jernbanegade.

Horsens for sites Nos. 2–4, 6, 10, 13, 15 and 16. Coach connection with almost any part of South-east Jutland. Tourist Information Office Kongensgade 25, opposite the railway station. Hotels: Bygholm Park Hotel; Jørgensens hotel, Søndergade 17; Missionshotellet, Gl. jernbanegade 6.

Area 5. North-West Jutland South of the Limfjord

1: Barde: near A15, 20 km west of Herning. Then south at the 20 km stone to Storhøj, a large Bronze Age barrow, which was excavated in the nineteenth century. It contained a plundered oak coffin. The finds (sword sheath, gold diadem, and two wooden bowls) are in the National Museum. Just north of A15 between the villages Vorgod and Abild is an earthen dyke, 600 m long, Bardedige, the age of which is uncertain.

2: Bregninggård: West of Herning along A 15, turn north along A11 and then east to Bregninggård (about 14 km north of the crossroads A15–A11). Passage grave built of eight uprights—the capstone was removed many years ago. There is free admittance to the chamber.

3: Fabjerg: About 6 km south-east of Lemvig, between Fabjerg Church and Savmansgård farm, is a beautiful group, or rather a row, of well preserved Bronze Age barrows placed along the prehistoric trackway leading to the west coast.

4: Finderup Rishøj: 15 km east of Ringkøbing by A15. Turn south at the 15 km stone and proceed for about 1 km to a group of six Bronze Age barrows among which is Finderup Rishøj—not less than 6 m high.

5: Fladhøj: About 10 km south of Lemvig by A11 and then eastwards to Flynder church. About 400 m south-west of the church is Fladhøj, dating from the Bronze Age. The finds from this barrow which was excavated in the 1860's consist of a wooden bowl, a bronze dagger, and fragments of woollen garments—now in the National Museum.

6: Gimsing: near Gimsinghoved farm, 1 km south of Struer, is a beautiful group of five barrows on a hill-top commanding a truly magnificent view of the surrounding scenery.

7: Hagebrogård: 25 km west of Viborg along A16 is Hagebro and just south of the road is a small passage grave with a chamber 4 m long built of nine uprights. The chamber was excavated in 1910 and yielded finds both from the Passage-Grave Culture and the Battle-Axe Culture. The finds are in the National Museum and specially noteworthy is a beautiful clay vessel, the Hagebrogård vessel, one of the finest Neolithic vessels from Denmark.

8: Hjortsballe barrows: From Herning to Arnborg by A18, in Arnborg turn north-west along the road through Høgildgård Plantation, in the north-western part of which are the Hjortsballe barrows—two well preserved large barrows probably of Bronze Age date.

9: Hygum: From Lemvig to Hove and then along the Harboøre road where, between Hygum and Engbjerg church, is a beautiful group of about thirty barrows mostly of Bronze Age date. The hills and the barrows command a fantastic view of the bleak coast and its sand dunes. The barrows were, unfortunately, seriously damaged by German defence works during the war.

10: Mangehøje: About 10 km north-west of Holstebro is Mangehøje Plantation. A group of twelve Bronze Age barrows is to be found in the eastern outskirts of the plantation.

11: Muldbjerg: About 8 km north of the crossroads A15–A11 in Muldbjerg village (also a railway station on the Ringkøbing–Holstebro line) is a fine long barrow, Muldhøje, 41 m long, originally two round barrows which were joined into one. The north-eastern barrow contained the famous man's garment from the Early Bronze Age, the Muldbjerg garment, which is now in the National Museum.

12: Mølbjerg: About 5 km west of Struer, south of Resen church, is Mølbjerg farm, in the fields of which there is a group of five fine Bronze Age barrows.

13: Rammedige: About 10 km south-west of Lemvig, by Rom and Ramme. 2 km west of Ramme station is the more than 400 m long Ramme dyke with an eastward facing ditch. The age of the dyke is uncertain but it is a fact that it is a blockade across the ancient east-west trackway of North-western Jutland (cf. No. 3). Between the dyke

Plate 4. The 'Store Døs' barrows near Maabjerg (Area 5, No. 14)

and Dybe church is a fine group of thirteen barrows. Tradition tells that the dyke was built as a defence against an English king, Angel, and that the surrounding barrows cover the dead bodies of those who fell in the fight against him.

14: Store Døs: A group of barrows between Måbjerg and Navr. Måbjerg is 2 km north of Holstebro. On the Måbjerg side of the small stream Ellebæk is a group of eighteen barrows, most of them from the Bronze Age; two of them are flat-topped and of grand dimensions. On the Navr side of the stream are three long barrows, one of these not less than 96 m long. All these barrows were placed along the ancient trackway to the west coast (cf. No. 3 and 13).

15: Tinghøje: 12 km from Holstebro by A16, turn north at Borbjerg plantation and proceed to Stendis moor. Tinghøje is a fine group of six barrows.

16: Trehøje: About 20 km north-west of Herning. From Herning to Timring and then further west through Najbjerg to Trehøje, which is a fine group of barrows on top of a heather-grown hill which commands a fine view of the vast, flat stretches of former moorland, just recently cultivated.

17: Ølstrup: By A15 from Ringkøbing, after 9.5 km turn northwards to Ølstrup (3 km from A15, also railway station on the line Ringkøbing–Holstebro). In a field east of the church is a group of one round and one long barrow and two long dolmens. The long barrow contained an Early Neolithic burial, the round barrow a burial belonging to the Battle-Axe Culture. One long dolmen is 58 m long and has three chambers; the other is 32 m long with one chamber. The finds from these barrows were excavated in the 1930's and are in the National Museum.

18: Øster Lem Moor: From Ringkøbing by A15 and along the Skjern road to Sønder Lem church and from here to Løvstrup plantation; south of this road is a stretch of moorland with well-preserved Iron Age fields.

Ringkøbing Museum has the best prehistoric collection within the area. Especially noteworthy is the material from the Early Iron Age settlement at Fjand. Open May–November, 10 a.m.–6 p.m.; November–May Wednesdays and Sundays 2–4 p.m.

Skjern Museum has a small collection of local finds. Open during the summer season from 3.30–5.30 p.m.

Herning Museum is the largest in the district, but the archaeological collection is small as the speciality of this museum is local peasant culture.

Holstebro Museum has a good collection of Mesolithic (Gudenå) culture and Neolithic finds (Battle-Axe Culture). Open daily from 3–6 p.m. except Mondays.

Lemvig Museum, Vestergade, has a good local collection. Open June–August on Wednesdays, Fridays and Sundays from 3–5 p.m. The rest of the year Wednesdays and Sundays from 3–5 p.m.

Struer Museum, Søndergade 23, has a small prehistoric collection. Open daily from 2–4 p.m. Sundays also 10–12 a.m.

Ringkøbing is well suited for visits to the sites Nos. 1, 4, 11, 17 and 18 (Nos. 1, 4 and 11 might just as well be approached from Herning). Good coach connections to the neighbouring towns. Tourist Information Office at Torvegade. Hotels: Jernbanehotellet, Østergade 54; Ringkøbing, Torvet; Missionshotellet, Torvet 8.

Herning for sites Nos. 2, 8 and 16. The coach station is at Jernbanegade. Tourist Information Office: Bredgade 20. Hotels: Eyde, Torvet; Prinsen, Banegårdspladsen; Hotel Herning, Østergade 32; Centralhotellet, Bredgade 45; Missionshotellet, Bredgade 20; Højskolehjemmet, Bredgade 30.

Lemvig for sites Nos. 3, 5, 9 and 13. The coach station is at Østergade 55, Tourist Information Office at the harbour. Hotels: Jespersens hotel, Søndergade; Lemvig Missionshotellet, Østergade 16.

Struer for sites Nos. 6 and 12. Coaches run to Holstebro, Lemvig, Thisted and Hvidbjerg. Tourist Information Office: Østergade 31. Hotels: Grand, Østergade 24; Stigaard's Hotel, Østergade 30; Carlsen's Hotel, Østergade 54.

Holstebro for sites Nos. 7, 10, 14 and 15. Coach service to several towns in West Jutland. The coach station is at Nørreport. Tourist Information Office, Nørregade 51. Hotels: Schaumburg, Nørregade 26; Knudsen's Hotel, Nørregade 40; Missionshotellet ved Nørreport.

Area 6. Central Jutland and the Peninsular Salling

1: **Bigum:** From Viborg by A16 and then by Tjele and Vammen to Bigum; 2 km north of the village, east of Bigumgård farm is a passage grave 4 m long and 2.5 m broad. The chamber was excavated in 1914 and yielded finds both from the Passage-Grave and the Battle-Axe Cultures. Among the clay vessels is one of the very few bell-beakers found in Denmark. The finds are in the National Museum.

2: **Fly Moor:** 6 km south of Skive several Early Iron Age fields are to be seen; the best are east and south-east of Svansø. Excavations have dated the fields to the Celtic Iron Age (100 B.C.–0).

3: **Glyngøre:** Thirteen large Bronze Age barrows south of Glyngøre, near the ferry at Pinen (see also Area 10), perched high in the hilly countryside facing Sallingsund, the narrow strait between Salling and Mors.

4: **Grensten church:** About 8 km south-west of Randers. A rune-stone, the original finding-place of which is unknown, is placed between the tower and the nave. The inscription reads, 'Toke, the blacksmith, erected this stone to Revle, son of Esge Bjørn's son. God help their soul'.

5: **Havredal plantation:** South of Viborg by A13 to Lysgård and then south-west to Sjørup. In the eastern outskirts of the plantation are thirty-eight barrows scattered over a stretch of 2 km.

6: **Hjermind:** 20 km east of Viborg. From Viborg to Bjerringbro (by road or railway) and then 3 km north-east to Hjermind. In the rectory garden is a rune-stone. On the back is an engraving of a ship; the text on the front reads, 'Tholv erected this stone to his brother Rade a most well-bred man'.

Plate 5. Stone cist of Roman Iron Age date from Løvel Vandmølle, near Viborg (Area 6, No. 7). Photographed during the excavation

7: Løvel Vandmølle (water-mill): 10 km north of Viborg by A13 and then 1 km west to the water-mill. Stone cist from the Roman Iron Age, a form of burial characteristic of North Jutland (especially Himmerland and Vendsyssel). The chamber is 3 m long and 1.5 m broad, built of twenty-six uprights in two layers; three capstones are preserved. The finds from the chamber—a fine set of pottery vessels—are in the National Museum.

8: Skern: About 23 km east of Viborg on the Viborg-Randers road. Rune-stone placed in the cemetery. The inscription reads, 'Sasgerd, Finulv's daughter, erected the stone to Odinkar, Osbjørn's (?) son, the precious and loyal. A witch the man who ruins this memorial'. A mask with an ornamental, interlaced beard adorns the stone.

Just north of the river valley, just east of the church is a dolmen with a square chamber built of four uprights.

9: **Sødal wood:** Some 8 km north-east of Viborg, just north of Rødding, the road from Rødding to Vrå passes through Sødal wood. Near the road are two well-preserved barrows and a dolmen chamber. In the eastern part of the wood is a bauta-stone 1.5 m high and a small dolmen built of three uprights On the road from Rødding to Vammen, north of the road, is a small barrow covering two passage graves.

10: **Sønder Vinge church:** About 5 km south-east of Skern. A rune-stone is placed in the nave of the parish church. The inscription reads, '. . . erected this stone to his two brothers Urøke and Kade . . . sowed and practised sorcery. A witch the man who ruins this memorial'.

11: **Tastum sø** (lake): About 8 km south-east of Skive, south of the former, now drained and cultivated, Tastum lake, and west of Kardyb farm is a magnificent long dolmen, 185 m long, the largest in Jutland. 2 km south-east of Tastum is a group of barrows, Hvalshøje, the south-eastern most of these covers a double passage grave, the chambers of which are about 3 m long.

12: **Ulstrup:** 20 km south-west of Randers (on the road to Bjerringbro) is Ulstrup Manor. In the park, near the road, is a rune-stone, the fragmentary inscription on which reads, '. . . erected (this stone) to his "Skippers" Thire and Tue'.

13: **Ulvedal plantation:** About 20 km south-west of Viborg on the Karup–Torning road. In the centre of the plantation is a magnificent long barrow, 36 by 7.5 m with 62 peristaliths and two stone cists measuring 3.5 by 1.25 m. The cists have yielded finds from the Late Neolithic period which are now in the National Museum. The popular name of the monument is 'Jens Langknivs Hule' (i.e. Jens Long-knife's burrow). Jens Langkniv was a notorious highwayman who lived in the seventeenth century.

14: **Øster Bjærgegrav church:** On A16, 9 km west of Randers. In the church are two rune-stones. The larger, the top of which is missing, carries the fragmentary inscription, 'Tove had this stone made to her husband Tomme (a well-bred) Thegn. He . . . Tvegge Hén'. The smaller stone is better preserved, the inscription reads. 'Gyde had this stone made to her husband Thorbjørn, a most well-bred Thegn. And Thord carved these runes'.

15: **Ålum church**: 10 km west of Randers on the Randers–Viborg road running south of A16. Four rune-stones are placed in and near the church. The larger of the two stones in the cemetery has the inscription, 'Vigot erected this stone to his son Esge, God help his soul well'. On the back of the stone is a fragmentary carving of a mounted warrior. The text of the smaller stone is, 'Tyre, Vigot's wife, had this stone erected to Torbjørn, Sibbe's son her cousin, whom she loved better than (had he been her) own son'. This inscription is most unusual as it is the only Viking Age inscription which reveals warmer, human feelings. Inside the church, the larger stone carries the text, 'Tole erected this stone to his son Ingeld, a most well-bred man'. The smaller stone is only a fragment, the inscription of which is too fragmentary to give sense.

The principal museum of this area is Viborg Stiftsmuseum (at the old Town Hall) with very good collections from Central Jutland, especially from the Battle-Axe Culture. Open during the summer season from 10–12 noon and from 1.30–5 p.m. except Mondays; during the winter season Wednesdays, Saturdays and Sundays from 1.30–5 p.m.

Skive Museum, near the harbour, has an excellent prehistoric collection, noteworthy is the Neolithic Mollerup find with not less than 13,000 amber beads.

Klosterlund Museum has a good Mesolithic collection from the many sites in Central Jutland, especially the Gudenå Culture.

Viborg is a good starting point to the sites Nos. 1, 5–10 and 13 (sites Nos. 8 and 10 can just as well be reached from Randers) with good coach and train connections. The Tourist Information Office is at Dankirkestræde 4. Hotels: Phoenix, Sct Mathiasgade 21; Missionshotellet, Sct Mathiasgade 5; Højskolehotellet, Sct Mathiasgade 12; Motel Viborg, Koldingvej 115.

Randers is well suited for the sites Nos. 4, 8, 10, 12, 14 and 15. About Randers, see Area 7.

Skive is a good starting point for sites Nos. 2, 3, and 11. The coach station is at Søndergade and the Tourist Information Office at Posthustorvet. Hotels: Royal, Østergade 5; Gammel Skivehus, Østerskov (a cuisine speciality is eels from Flyndersø); Grand Hotel, Østerbro 14.

Area 7. The Peninsula Djursland

1: Assens: 6 km east of Mariager. Just south of the town is a group of ten barrows and a stone circle. West of the town is a smaller group of two long barrows and one round barrow, Baunehøj. North of the road to Hadsund, not far from Baunehøj, is a fine passage grave built of eight uprights and with a long passage.

2: Balle: 10 km from Grenå by A15 and then through Lund to Balle and Hoed villages. Near Balle railway station is a small passage grave and east of Balle is a fine group of four Bronze Age barrows.

3: Barkær: 20 km from Grenå by A15 to Tåstrup and then north to Barkær and Tåstrup plantation, where a fine round dolmen is to be seen.

4: Dalbyover: About 20 km east of Mariager either by the road to Kastbjerg or the road through Skrødstrup and Kærby. In the parish church is a rune-stone with the following inscription, 'Tue, Kitu's son, erected [this stone to] his friend, Thorgny's fosterchild(?)'.

5: Ebeltoft: On the peninsula south of Ebeltoft are several fine groups of barrows. 4 km south of the town near the village of Elsegårde are three groups of ten, five, and three barrows and at Boeslum (2 km east of Ebeltoft) two barrows on a hill-top and further east, near the harbour, are three barrows.

6: Emmedsbro plantation: About 15 km north of Grenå near the north coast of Djursland. Several Bronze Age barrows and megaliths. In the north-western part, near the coast, is a group of twelve barrows, and on the coast, west of the wood, is a long dolmen with one chamber.

7: Fyrkat: 4 km south-west of Hobro. Viking fortress. Sixteen houses exactly alike are surrounded by a circular wall with four gates facing north, west, east and south. The houses were built of wood and the wall was strengthened by strong palisades. Fyrkat is smaller than the similar fortress, Trelleborg, in South Zealand (Sjælland) (see Area 18, No. 36). Only three of the four sections of the fortress have been excavated, the fourth is kept intact for future research.

8: Glenstrup church: 5 km south of Hobro by A10 and then 2 km east, south of Glenstrup lake. A rune-stone is placed in the porch of the parish church, the inscription reads, 'Toke erected this memorial to his father Uflå (?), a most well-bred Thegn'.

9: Hillested: 18 km from Grenå by A15 to Tirstrup and then about 5 km to the south-east is Hillested village around which are several prehistoric monuments. On the road to Sønderskov are a round dolmen and a dolmen chamber with a large capstone. Two km south of Hillested is the Hulgade farm, near this are a round dolmen and a long dolmen with two chambers. In the southern part of Sønderskov is a group of eight Bronze Age barrows.

10: Hobro–Mariager: The road (about 12 km) from Hobro to Mariager is almost bordered by fine megalithic monuments. At Katbjerg, north of the road, are Jordhøj and Ormehøj. Ormehøj has an oval chamber, 5 m long, and behind this a smaller chamber, a feature which is very rare and only found in north Jutland. Jordhøj has a passage 6 m long and a small oval chamber. Both passage graves were excavated in the 1890's; the finds are in the National Museum. Further east is a small passage grave without capstones and just inside the drive to 'Voldstedlund' is one of the most imposing Danish long dolmens. The peristaliths are up to 3 m high and the two chambers are of grand proportions, one of them has uprights of more than 2 m height. The dolmen was partly excavated in 1960. The finds—fine pottery from the Middle Neolithic period—are in the National Museum.

11: Kolind church: About 20 km west of Grenå by Vejlby, Lyngby, and Albøge. In the porch of the parish church is a rune-stone, the inscription on which reads, 'Toste, Asved's blacksmith, erected this stone to his brother Tue who died in the East' (i.e. Russia).

12: Laurbjerg: 15 km south-west of Randers. In the porch of the parish church is a rune-stone the inscription on which reads, 'Bolnød's true stone. Ville.' (i.e. Ville is the name of the person who carved the runes).

Plate 6. The beautiful round dolmen near Knebel, Mols (Area 7, No. 15)

Just north of the town between the railway and the road is a dolmen chamber surrounded by a low mound, and nearer to the road (by the 15 km stone) is a large barrow.

13: **Mariager:** 1 km east of Mariager is the large Bronze Age barrow Hohøj, placed high on top of a hill with a lovely view of the fjord and the surrounding scenery. A few km to the south-west are Hem and Skrødstrup woods with several groups of barrows. In the northern part of Hem wood is a fine long barrow, and in the western outskirts of Skrødstrup wood are four barrows, the Bøggild barrows, and in the eastern part of the wood is a fine group of seven barrows.

14: **Mellerup:** About 14 km north-east of Randers by the road to Harreslev and Tvede. Between Hungstrup wood and Skalmstrup village are two stones with cup-marks, one is found just east of the navigation mark, the other is nearer to Tvede very near a long dolmen with one rectangular chamber. In the north-western part of Hungstrup wood is a fine group of thirteen Bronze Age barrows.

15: **Mols** is the western peninsula on the south coast of Djursland. A beautiful, hilly and heathergrown district rich in prehistoric monuments. The gem is the round dolmen, Knebeldyssen, one of the finest round dolmens in Denmark, situated 2 km south of Agri village. The dolmen has twenty-three peristaliths of truly magnificent dimensions forming a circle of 20 m in diameter; the chamber is built of five uprights and one gigantic capstone. On the road to Agri from the Knebel dolmen are three dolmens one of which has a polygonal chamber with cup-marks on the capstone.

Further south from Agri to Knebel Vig are the villages Strands and Torup, between these villages is a fine dolmen with a polygonal chamber and a large capstone. Just west of Torup is another dolmen with a square chamber and cup-marks on the capstone.

One km north-west of Agri is a fine group of Bronze Age barrows, Stabelhøje, perched high on the hill-tops which command a magnificent view of sea and countryside. Julingshøje, 2 km north-east of Agri, is another fine group of Bronze Age barrows and to the south, on the road to Vistoft, are three Bronze Age barrows, Trehøje, crowning the heathergrown hill-tops, they are the most magnificent in a group of twelve barrows.

16: Ramten–Tostrup–Nimtofte: 16 km west of Grenå on A16. Just south of the road is a dolmen with a polygonal chamber and a large capstone. Further south, on the road to Tøstrup, is a fine group of megaliths. Beside the road is a round dolmen with many peristaliths and a polygonal chamber. West of the road is a round dolmen with a pentagonal chamber, and near Lykkeslund farm three dolmens: a long dolmen with three chambers, a round dolmen with a pentagonal chamber, and a long dolmen with three chambers, a round dolmen with a pentagonal chamber, and a long dolmen with a rectangular chamber. Beside the road through Sivested to Nimtofte are several fine groups of Bronze Age barrows and just south of Nimtofte a long dolmen and a triangular stone enclosure probably of Late Iron Age date. Halfway between Nimtofte and Ramten, close to the railway, is a large barrow covering a passage grave.

17: Rimsø church: About 10 km north-west of Grenå. In the cemetery is a flat-topped barrow, probably of Iron Age date; on top of this barrow is a rune-stone with the rather enigmatic inscription, 'Thore, Enrådes brother, erected this stone to his mother and . . . ku . . . aubi as worst for the son (?)'.

18: Rønde: About 15 km north-west of Ebeltoft. South of Rønde are two small woods on either side of the road, Hestehaven and Ringelmose wood, in the latter are seven dolmens, among which a fine round dolmen and a long dolmen with a pentagonal chamber. Just north of the wood and east of the road, are three dolmens, the one in the middle of this small group is a fine long dolmen with a hexagonal chamber. In Hestehaven wood are two Bronze Age barrows placed in the north-western part, examples of the very rare stone-built barrows, or cairns. In the southern part of Hestehaven is a long dolmen with two chambers. Further south, near the coast, are three Late Neolithic stone cists.

19: Spentrup: 10 km north of Randers by the Randers–Mariager road, turn east to Spentrup at Hastrup village. In the wall surrounding the cemetery, near the gate, is a rune-stone the inscription of which reads, 'May these runes live long'. A ship is carved in the stone.

20: Stabrand, 15 km north of Ebeltoft (either by Feldballe or Tirstrup), is rich in megalithic monuments. North of Stabrand is a group of fifteen dolmens among which Mejlkirken is a fine monument with its large chamber covered with a magnificent capstone. On the Stabrand–Nødager road stands the farm Skeldrup, near this are a round dolmen with a pentagonal chamber and two long dolmens with one chamber each. At Mårup, on the Feldballe–Kolind road, are a long dolmen with three chambers and a round dolmen with well-preserved peristaliths and a covered chamber.

21: Stenvad: About 15 km west of Grenå by A16 to Ørum and 3 km north-west to Stenvad. Between Stenvad and Ulstrup are several megalithic monuments, five long dolmens and one round dolmen. North-west of Stenvad on a patch of moorland is another group of three dolmens; one of these, a fine long dolmen with two chambers, is depicted on the back of our 50 kr notes. On small islands in the peat-bogs west of Stenvad are several (rather inaccessible) dolmens, the finest of these is in Horsemose (about 1 km west of the '50 kr dolmen')—a long dolmen with three chambers. Further west in the southern part of the bog Fuglsø mose, near Kvarsbrogård farm, is a fine well-preserved dolmen with an intact circle of peristaliths and a covered chamber.

22: Trustrup: 23 km from Randers by A16 to Avning, from Avning about 12 km to Tustrup by Gesing and Nørager. Tustrup is a mega-lithic monument comprising two dolmens, a passage grave, and cult house for religious ceremonies placed in the centre of the area. The cult house is of horseshoe shape built of slabs. The passage grave has a chamber 10 m long and a smaller chamber behind this. This complex was excavated in the 1950's and it was proved that all the monuments date from the same period within the Middle Neolithic Age. The rich finds, especially pottery of excellent quality, are in the Prehistoric Museum of Århus.

23: Vester Tørslev: 8 km south-east of Hobro. In the porch of the parish church is a rune-stone which was found at Getrup in 1870. The inscription reads, 'Hala, Iitu's son, erected this stone to his brother Asulv (?)'.

24: Vindblæs: 15 km east of Mariager. An area with many Bronze Age barrows. Ecst of the road to Hadsund is Lystrup plantation with a fine group of barrows in the north-eastern part and in the southern part is the well-preserved large barrow, Hanehøj; west of the plantation are two long barrows placed on either side of the road. 1 km south of Vindblæs church near Vindbjerggård farm is a beautiful group of seven barrows; the largest one is not less than 6 m high.

25: Øster Alling: 20 km south-east of Randers, by A16 to Drastrup (10 km) and then south-east to Øster Alling by Hørning and Vester Alling. In the porch of the parish church is a rune-stone with the inscription, 'Thore erected this stone to Fastuld Myge'.

Randers Museum is the principal museum of this area.

Djursland Museum at Grenå, Søndergade 1, has a good prehistoric collection especially of the Stone and Iron Age finds. Open during the summer from 2–5 p.m.

Hobro Museum is at 'The Dower House', Vestergade. The prehistoric collection is rather small, but some of the finds from the Fyrkat fortress are on permanent loan from the National Museum.

Mariager is the prettiest little fairy-tale town imaginable and a good starting point for the sites Nos. 1, 4, 10, 13 and 24 (site No. 10 can as well be approached from Hobro). Coaches run to Hobro and Hadsund, Gerlev, Randers and Assens. The Tourist Information Office is at the Mariager Bookshop and the railway station. Hotels: Mariager at Østergade and Postgården.

Randers is well situated for the sites Nos. 11, 12, 14, 19, 22 and 23. The coach station is at Østervold. Excellent coach and railway connections to almost any part of Jutland. The Tourist Information Office is at Helligåndshuset, Erik Menvedsplads 1. Hotels: Hotel Randers; Missionshotellet Ansgar, Jernbanegade 16; Højskolehotellet, Middelgade 6; Vesterport, Vestergade 66; Westend, Vestergade 53.

Hobro is well situated for the sites Nos. 7, 8, 10 and 23. The coach station is at Biesgade. Excellent coach and railway connections. The Tourist Information Office is at Adelgade 23. Hotels: Grand Hotel, Adelgade 54; Højskolehjemmet, Adelgade 56. Do not miss Bech's konditori (the Danish equivalent of tea-shop); they serve excellent pastry.

Granå is a good starting point for the sites Nos. 2, 3, 9, 10, 16, 17 and 21. (Site No. 9 is just as easily approached from Ebeltoft.) 28 km from Tirstrup Airport, daily flights from Copenhagen and Ålborg. The coach station is at the railway station. (Grenå is connected by ferry to Hundested with train connection from Copenhagen and Hillerød.) The Tourist Bureau is at Mogensgade 2. Hotels: Du Nord; Dagmar, Storegade 2; Grenå Missionshotel, Storegade 9.

Ebeltoft is another picturesque little town, well worth a visit. Only 13 km from Tirstrup Airport. Coach connections to Femmøller–Rønde–Århus; Tirstrup–Kolind; Rønde–Mørke–Randers and Helgenæs–Knebel. Hotels: Hvide Hus. Skansen at Nedergade and Vigen, Adelgade 5. A good country inn is Molskroen, 2 km east of Femmøller. Site No. 19 might just as well be approached from Hvidsten kro (inn) as from Randers. Hvidsten kro, on the Randers–Mariager road 11 km north of Randers, was during the war a centre of the local resistance movement. In 1944 the innkeeper, Marius Fiil, was executed by the Germans together with his son and son-in-law and six other patriots from the neighbourhood.

Area 8. Himmerland (North-East Jutland, South of the Limfjord)

1: Albæk: 2 km east of A13, 10 km from Støvring station. In the plantation are several Bronze Age barrows and two stone circles built of a hundred and forty and fifty stones; their date is uncertain.

2: Alhøj: About 27 km north of Viborg by A16; then where A16 crosses Simested å take the road going south-east toward Hvilsom. About 1 km from the crossroads is Alhøj, a dolmen built of five solid uprights and one capstone.

3: Borremose: 4 km south-east of Års. In the bog, Borremose, is a fortified stronghold—a refuge dating from the early Celtic Iron Age. A small island in the bog was surrounded by an earthwall and a ditch. The stronghold was given up and fell into disrepair, but in the later part of the Celtic Iron Age the island was once again inhabited. This time a cobbled road led across the bog to the island where about 20 farm houses were built—of the usual early Iron Age pattern: rectangular, with the cow-byre in the eastern half and living quarters in the western half.

Borremose is restored after extensive excavations in the 1930's, but as a compromise between the two phases: the dyke and ditch belong to the earlier phase and the houses which are laid out with low turf walls are from the later phase. The finds from Borremose are in the National Museum.

4: Buderup: On A10 about 30 km south of Ålborg. At the crossroads (south of Støvring) of A10 and the Nibe road is a small area with deep cart-tracks from a prehistoric road.

5: Disterhøje: About 8 km west of Hobro beside the Ålestrup–Gedsted road. In one of the barrows called Disterhøje is a large Late Neolithic stone cist, 6.5 m long and 2.5 m broad, with a small ante-chamber. The large stone cists are very characteristic features of the Late Neolithic period in North-East Jutland.

Plate 7. The stronghold and village, Borremose, from the Celtic Iron Age. Air photograph of the restored site (Area 8, No. 3)

6: Ellidshøj (also written Elleshøj): About 13 km south of Ålborg by A10 (or by railway). In the centre of the town is a megalithic burial, an octagonal chamber with one capstone.

7: Ertebølle: The classical 'kitchen-midden' which has given its name to the whole Late Mesolithic Culture. The site is protected by The Ancient Monuments Act. 18 km south of Løgstør, then west to Ertebølle village. The shell-mound is placed between the low-lying beach and the higher land behind, i.e. just at the ancient (litorina) beach. Ertebølle was excavated in the 1890's and the finds are in the National Museum.

8: Ettrup: About 25 km west of Hobro by the road to Ålestrup, then south to Fjelsø and then Ettrup is 2 km further south. Ettrup is a double passage grave with two chambers and two passages. The chambers were excavated in 1932 and the finds—amber beads—are in the National Museum.

9: Farsø church: In the porch of the parish church is a rune-stone with the inscription, 'Toste and Asbjørn erected this stone to their brother Tue'.

10: Ferslev church: 13 km south of Ålborg by the road east of A10. In the porch is a rune-stone with the inscription, 'Toke, Lutaris son erected this stone to his son Åste'.

11: Fjelsø: (See also No. 8) south-west of Fjelsø are two large barrows, one contains a passage grave with a small extra chamber adjoined. The main chamber is 4 m long and 2 m broad. Excavated by the National Museum in 1920; outside the entrance several potsherds were found.

12: Flejsborg: Halfway between Års and Løgstør. About 1 km north-east of the village is a small stone cist from the Late Neolithic period, only 2 m long and 0.5 m broad. The finds from this burial are in Vesthimmerlands Museum, Års.

13: Giver church: 6 km north-east of Års. The rune-stone in the porch was once the threshold of the church door. The inscription reads, 'Karl erected this stone to his father Torsten, a most well-bred Thegn'.

14: Gunderup church: 15 km south-east of Ålborg on the Ålborg–Hadsund road. One of the two rune-stones in the porch was found on a barrow at Fjalrø field. The inscription reads, 'Toke erected these stones to his relative (or brother-in-law) Ebbe, a well-bred Thegn, and to his mother Tove. They both lie in this mound. Ebbe bequeathed his (worldly) goods to Toke'. The other stone in the porch is said to come from a field belonging to the rectory; its inscription reads, 'Østen erected this stone to his father Asulv'.

15: Hvilsom: 13 km west of Hobro, south of the church, just north of the country lane leading west is a small barrow with a Late Neolithic stone cist, 2.8 m long and 1.7 m broad. 2.5 km south-west of Hvilsom and about 200 m south of the road to Støttrup is a Bronze Age barrow connected to a stone circle by a row of stones.

16: Jægersborg skov (wood) is the eastern part of the vast Rold skov. East of the road from Skørping to Astrup, 3 km south of Skørping is one of the large Late Neolithic stone cists, not less than 5 m long and 3.4 m broad, built of thirteen uprights and four capstones.

17: Lovns: About 25 km west of Hobro, beautifully situated in picturesque scenery is a small circular wall surrounded by a ditch. The age of this monument is uncertain.

18: 'Mulle's grav' (i.e. tomb): About 10 km west of Ålborg by the Nibe road to Frejlev, then south to Svendstrup Vestergårde. Halfway to the latter village is the so-called 'Mulle's tomb'—an imposing long barrow of 70 m length; it may be a long dolmen with completely covered chambers.

19: Myrhøj: 18 km south of Løgstør. In the fork between the road to Løgstør and the road to Ertebølle (see No. 7) is a stone cist built of six uprights and three capstones. This cist dates from the Roman Iron Age —such stone cists are the most common burials of this period in North Jutland—the finds, two iron knives and seven clay vessels, are in Vesthimmerlands Museum, Års.

20: Møldrup: A small village about 8 km south-east of Skørping. About 1 km north-west of the village are two stone cists dating from the Roman Iron Age, both are about 2.5 m long and about 2 m broad.

21: Ravnkilde church: North-west of Hobro. 10 km by A10, then north-west at Vebbestrup past Nysum to Ravnkilde. In the garden wall of the rectory is a rune-stone which was found on a small barrow at Lille Rørbæk. The inscription reads, 'Asgot, Thygote's son, erected this stone to his brother Esge'. On a barrow by the church is another rune-stone, which was excavated in the 1850's. The inscription reads, 'Asser, estate agent, Kugge's son, carved these runes to queen Asbod'.

22: Skivum: 6 km north-west of Års, 3 km south-east of Skivum is a stone cist and two small barrows. The cist is built of fourteen stones; it is 2 m long and 1.2 m broad.

23: Skivum church: In the porch of the parish church is a rune-stone which was found in the cemetery wall. The inscription reads, 'The mother Tyre and the sons Odinkar and Gudmund, those three erected these memorials to Ki . . . (?) the huppska (?) he was the first and best of landsmen in Denmark'.

24: Skørbæk moor: About 10 km south-west of Nibe. Only a small patch is left of the former Skørbæk moor between Gundersted and Skørbæk hedehuse (hedehuse: a village on the moor); on this stretch of moorland are several Iron Age fields and traces of six houses. The date of the village is Late Celtic and Early Roman Iron Age, it was excavated in the 1930's and the finds are in Vesthimmerland's Museum, Års.

25: Sohngårdsholm: In the eastern outskirts of Ålborg. A stone cist from the Roman Iron Age built of seven uprights and two capstones; the cist measures 2.3 by 1.8 m. The finds were five clay vessels which are in Ålborg Museum.

26: Spanskhøj: 8 km from Hobro, by the Ålestrup road to Hørby, then westwards to Snæbum. The barrow lies just north of the road from Snæbum to Hannerupgård. The barrow which is 4 m high and more than 20 m in diameter covers a double passage grave with oval chambers about 4 m in diameter. Both chambers were excavated in 1929 and the finds, flint axe and daggers, amber beads, and clay vessels, are in the National Museum.

North-east of Spanskhøj is another mound, 7.5 m high, which also covers a double passage grave, among the finest and best preserved in the country. Both chambers were excavated in the 1890's; flint blades, amber beads and potsherds were found, which are now in the National Museum.

27: Stenstuen (the stone chamber): About 17 km south of Ålborg by A10 to Elleshøj, then east to Mjels. Stenstuen is a large dolmen about 1 km south-east of Mjels. Only a few peristaliths are preserved; the chamber is built of five uprights and on the capstone are several cup-marks.

28: Store Restrup: About 12 km west of Ålborg on the Nibe road. By the road running south from St Restrup Dairy are two dolmen chambers built as flat graves. The chambers were found and excavated in 1958; the finds were only a few flint axes which are in Ålborg Museum.

29: Store Monshøj: 20 km south of Ålborg by the Hadsund road, past Lindenborg turn east to Komdrup and Sønder Kongerslev (also a station on the Ålborg–Hadsund railway). Store Monshøj is near the village, a long dolmen 65 m long with two chambers of which one is pentagonal; the other is not so well preserved—only four uprights are still standing.

30: Suldrup: About 15 km north-east of Års, beside A13. Where the road leads off to Suldrup parish church is the passage grave Stenshøj. The chamber is built of fourteen uprights and four capstones; it is 7 m long and 2.5 m broad. At the western side is a smaller chamber built of three uprights and one capstone. Outside the porch of Suldrup church is a rune-stone which was found in the cemetery in 1895. The inscription reads, 'Rysk erected (this stone) to his brother Ufejg'.

31: Svalhøjgård: 19 km east of Hobro to Vive and then northwards to Astrup. At Vive moor, east of the road, is one of the most splendid Late Neolithic stone cists, 3.4 m long and 2.6 m broad, built of eight uprights and three capstones. The cist was excavated in 1937; three flint daggers and two spearheads were found together with a bronze pin. The finds are in the National Museum.

32: Svanfolk: 5 km south-west of Sdr Kongerslev (see No. 29). Hesthøj is a long dolmen near the village of Svanfolk; the chamber is built of four uprights and the capstone has several cup-marks.

33: Sønderhede: About 8 km north-east of Års between Sønderup and Skivum at Sønderhede, east of the road, is a dolmen with a hexagonal chamber and a short passage.

34: Tostrup: 13 km west of Ålborg by the Nibe road, turn south to Tostrup. About 1.5 m north-west of Tostrup are two passage graves The northern passage grave has an oval chamber built of eleven uprights and three capstones. The southern passage grave is somewhat larger but not so well preserved; none of the capstones are left.

35: 'Troldkirken' (i.e. The troll's church): 13 km west of Ålborg by the Nibe road. Just before Sønderholm a long dolmen is seen north of the road. Troldkirken is a truly magnificent monument, one of our finest long dolmens, built on a hill-top with a lovely view of the

Limfjord and the countryside. The peristaliths are up to 2 m high. The chamber has a short passage, it is hexagonal and covered with a single capstone.

36: Valsgård: 6 km north-east of Hobro by the Hadsund road. A dolmen chamber built of four uprights and one capstone. 1 km east of Valsgård is the village Redsø, 1 km south-east of the village is a long dolmen with nineteen peristaliths and a chamber built of four uprights.

37: Ønskestenen: Just north of Skørping on the road to Buderupholm Manor is a fine hexagonal dolmen chamber with one capstone. It is said that wishes come true when money is placed in the chamber.

38: Østerbølle: 22 km west of Hobro on the Ålestrup road. 2 km north of the village Østerbølle is a stretch of moorland with seven Iron Age houses. The village comprises about twenty houses, vast stretches of fields, a well, and a small cemetery. The site was excavated in the 1930's, the finds—mostly pottery—date the village to the Celtic and Early Roman Iron Age. The finds are in Vesthimmerland's Museum, Års.

39: Års: In the cemetery is a rune-stone the inscription on which reads, 'Asser erected this stone to his master Valtoke. The stone speaks that it will stand here for long. It shall be named Valtoke's "varde"'.

40: Årupgård: About 8 km south-east of Løgstør by the road through Vindblæs, Årupgård is 2 km south of the village, west of the farm on the north bank of the stream is a group of three Bronze Age barrows, and about 1 km from the farm is a long dolmen, about 100 m long. Fifty-eight peristaliths are still standing.

The principal museum of the district is Ålborg Historiske Museum, Adelgade 48, with excellent prehistoric collections. Open during the summer season every day except Mondays from 2–5 p.m., Sundays also from 10–12 noon; during the winter season Wednesdays and Saturdays from 1–3 p.m., Sundays from 10–12 noon.

Vesthimmerland's Museum at Års has excellent collections from the Iron Age villages in western Himmerland. Open Sundays from 4–6 p.m. and also by appointment with the caretaker.

Ålborg is a good starting point for sites Nos. 4–6, 10, 14, 18, 28, 29,

32, 34 and 35 (site No. 4 can just as well be visited from Års). The coach station is at Jyllandsgade; the Tourist Information Office is at Vesterbro 5.

Choice of Hotels: Hvide Hus; Central Hotel, Vesterbro 38; Phønix, Vesterbro 77; Motel Europa at Elleshøj, 14 km south of Ålborg; Hafnia, John F. Kennedy's plads; King Frederik, Kongensgade 8; Missionshotelle Ansgar, Prinsensgade 14; Motel Ålborg, Scheelsminde, Hobrovej 135.

Års is well suited to sites Nos. 1–4, 9, 12, 13, 22, 30, 33, 39 (site No. 12 can just as well be reached from Løgstør). The coach station is at Himmerlandsgade and the Tourist Information Office at Himmerlandsgade 67. Års is a railway station on the lines Hobro–Ålestrup–Løgstør and Ålborg–Hvalpsund.

Hotels: Års Hotel, Himmerlandsgade 111 and Himmerland, Himmerlandsgade 23.

Nibe is well suited for site No. 24. The coach station is at Torvet; the Tourist Information Office is at Lille Algade (the bookshop).

Hotels: Hotel Nibe and Turisthotellet.

Løgstør is a good starting point for the sites Nos. 7, 12 and 40. The coach station is at the Western Railway station; the Tourist Information Office is at Østerbrogade 14.

Hotels: Hotel du Nord, Fjordsgade 56; Mikkelsen's hotel, Jernbandegade.

Hobro is well suited for sites Nos. 5, 8, 11, 15, 17, 26, 31, 36 and 38. About Hobro, see Area 7.

A good country hotel is Rold Storkro on A10 near Skørping station. The sites Nos. 16, 20, 21, 29, 32 and 37 can easily be visited from this place.

Area 9. Thy

1: Gettrup: Just west of the road from Gettrup to Vestervig (30 km south of Thisted) is a small group of Bronze Age barrows of which Kobbeshøj is the largest, 25 m in diameter and about 5 m high. South of this group is a stone cist covered by two capstones.

2: Hov kalkværk: 10 km north-east of Thisted by A11. A flint mine from the Early Neolithic period. About twenty-five vertical shafts have been registered and several of them were excavated in the 1950's. When a shaft struck a layer of flint horizontal galleries were laid out and the flint blocks removed with picks. When shafts and galleries had been exploited they were filled in with debris. This mine is one of the very few known in Denmark.

3: Hurup: 30 km south of Thisted by A11. In the cemetery is a fragmentary rune-stone. As all the lines of the inscription are damaged the text cannot be read with certainty, it may be something like 'Thormod, a well-bred man, erected these memorials to . . . . his father (or brother)'.

4: Højstrup: 20 km north-east of Thisted, by A11 to Østerild, then east and south by the road to Frøstrup. East of the road is a small patch of moorland with about twenty small barrows, four ship-formed burials and more than seventy bauta stones. Some of the burials have been excavated, they contained both inhumation and cremation graves dating from the Early Viking period, ninth century A.D.

5: Hørdum church: 18 km south of Thisted by A11. In the porch of the parish church is a stone from the Viking period showing Thor fishing for the Midgård Serpent—a popular legend of the ancient pagan religion. The stone was found in 1954 during restoration work. It had been used as the first step on the stairs leading to the tower.

6: Høverhøj is just north of the road from Kolby to Hørdum, one of the most impressive of the thousands of Bronze Age barrows to be found in this part of Jutland. It is 40 m in diameter and 9 m high. In the northern part was found a stone cist dating from the Early Bronze Age. 1 km to the north-east is a group of three barrows, two round and one long barrow.

7: Klovenhøj is 3 km south of Fjerritslev near Kettrup village. A large round mound measuring 21 m in diameter by 3 m high covers a passage grave; the chamber is built of ten uprights and two capstones. Thirty large peristaliths surround the mound.

8: Lundehøj: 26 km south of Thisted just east of A11. A large mound about 30 m in dimater covers one of the finest passage graves in North Jutland. The main chamber is 7.5 m long and 2.5 m broad. A smaller chamber behind the main chamber measures 2 × 2 m. The chamber was excavated in 1837 and 1890. The smaller chamber contained human bones, a battle-axe of stone and some potsherds.

9: Rønhede plantation: About 6 km north-east of Vestervig. Four fine barrows are placed in an east-west line; the westernmost of these, called Store Stevnshøj is about 6 m high and 26 m in diameter. One of the mounds is a long barrow 52 m long.

10: Skyum Bjerge: Skyum is a village about 15 km south of Thisted —by A11 to Harring and Stagstrup and then southwards to Skyum Bjerge. The hilly countryside near the coast is protected and scheduled by the Ancient Monuments Act. Within the area are seventeen Bronze Age barrows, only a fraction of the original amount of prehistoric monuments which once graced the scenery.

11: Thisted: In the western outskirts of Thisted, near the water tower, is a long barrow which was once the longest in Denmark, originally 175 m long. The demolished part contained a stone cist with relics from the Early Bronze Age.

12: Torsted: About 5 km west of Thisted. Near the road leading out of the village to the west are two long dolmens. The first, just north of the road, is about 60 m long. It has only a few peristaliths left and in the centre is a large stone, which may have been the capstone of a chamber. A few hundred meters to the west is another long dolmen, 108 m long and up to 2 m high. In the eastern end is a ruined chamber of which only two stones are left.

13: Troldsting is in the vast stretch of high, heathergrown sand dunes facing the bleak North Sea coast, 15 km west of Fjerritslev by A11 to Kvolsbjerge (just past the 30 km stone), and then straight north to Bulbjerg huse. In the centre of the area is a hill at the foot of which are several bauta stones, at the eastern end are one large and two smaller barrows, the larger barrow contained a stone cist from the Late Neolithic period. Within the area are several dwelling-sites from the Stone and Bronze Ages.

14: Vang church: About 15 km west of Thisted. In the porch of the parish church is a rune-stone which originally came from Sjørring in 1741; it was known to be placed outside Sjørring cemetery. The inscription reads, 'Åse erected this stone to her husband Ødmund who was Finulv's housecarl'.

15: Vestervig: About 1.5 km north of Vestervig is Vestervig parish church—one of the largest in the country; now only a parish church but during the Middle Ages the centre of the then diocese. Opposite the church are the remains of one of the largest Iron Age villages in Jutland. More than fifty houses were excavated during the years 1962–5. A few of the houses have been preserved within a protected area. Especially interesting are the cobbled lanes between the houses. The village was inhabited from about the birth of Christ to the fourth century A.D. The finds from Vestervig are in the National Museum.

16: Ydby Hede (moor): About 8 km south-east of Vestervig, a few km east of A11, where the signpost indicates 'Oldtidskirkegården' (i.e. The prehistoric cemetery). A beautiful stretch of hilly moorland undisturbed from time immemorial, with imposing Bronze Age barrows and intersected with the deep cart-tracks of prehistoric lanes. Thirty-two barrows lie within the protected area which is—together with the surrounding countryside—one of the districts richest in prehistoric monuments to be found in Thy.

The principal museum of this area is Thisted Museum, Jernbanegade (just north-east of the church). The prehistoric collection is very good; the Bronze Age especially is well represented with many grave finds.

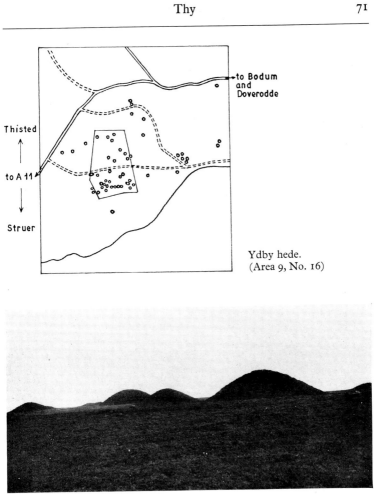

Ydby hede.
(Area 9, No. 16)

Plate 8. Bronze Age barrows within the protected area of Ydby hede (Area 9, No. 16, see also map above).

Thisted, the capital of Thy, is well suited for visits to the sites Nos. 2, 4–6, 10–12, and 14. The coach station is opposite the railway station; the town has excellent coach and train connections. Tourist information may be obtained at the Library and at the bookshop on Store Torv.

Hotels: Ålborg, Storegade 29; Afholdshotellet, Rosenkranzgade 14; Phoenix, Banegårdspladsen; Royal, Store Torv.

Vestervig is well suited for visits to the sites Nos. 1, 3, 8, 9, 15 and 16. Coach connections to Thisted–Hurup, Thisted–Hvidbjerg–Struer, Hurup–Agger, and Ydby. The nearest railway station is at Hurup.

Hotels: Vestervig Hotel. Morupmølle kro is a good country inn about 6 km north of Vestervig.

Fjerritslev on the border of Vendsyssel is well suited for visits to the sites Nos. 7 and 13. The town has good coach connections and a railway station on the Ålborg–Thisted line.

Fjerritslev Hotel is at Vestergade.

Area 10. The Islands Mors and Fur

Mors:

1: Legindbjerge: South of Nykøbing Mors on the west coast of the island. In a small wood on hilly ground (protected area) are several Bronze Age barrows and groups of barrows. On the moor west of the wood is a group of fourteen barrows, east of this is another of nine barrows.

2: Redsted: On the road from Nykøbing to Næssund between Vils and Hvidbjerg are several imposing Bronze Age barrows on both sides of the road. South of Vils is a group of three barrows; a little further west is the grandiose Malhøj placed on top of one of the highest points of Mors which commands a beautiful view of the island. Just off the road is Sønderherreds plantation with many Bronze Age barrows. The road to Rakkeby passes through the plantation, near the road is the barrow Kløvenhøj.

3: Salgjers høj: The road from Sdr. Dråby to Sun dbypasses the highest point of the island (89 m), on top of the hill is Salgjers høj and in the neighbourhood several other barrows such as Dejbjerg and Langbjerghøj.

4: Tæbring: North of Rakkeby on the southern coast of Dragstrup Vig is a passage grave built of ten uprights and one capstone. The passage grave is covered with an earth mound.

Fur:

1: Debel: Near the village are two smaller barrows, in one of them can be seen four capstones of a cist. Near these two barrows is a third of larger size, called Manhøj.

2: Smediehøje: Four Bronze Age barrows, the easternmost group of barrows on the hilly north coast of Fur.

3: Stendalhøje: South of Smediehøje, three barrows bear the name of Stendalhøje and two are called Odinshøje.

Mors can be reached by ferry from Salling, either Glyngøre–Nykøbing or Pinen–Plagen south of Glyngøre. From Thy there is a ferry across Næssund to Næs and the bridge from Vilsund to the Sundby road.

Nykøbing is the principal town. Hotels: Bendix' Hotel, Kirketorvet; Hamlet, Vestergade 8; Markvarsens Hotel and several smaller hotels and restaurants. The museum is at Dueholm kloster (monastery), collections of prehistoric finds, church inventory, and agriculture—all from the island of Mors. The coach station at Nykøbing runs a great many routes both on the island and to Thisted and Skive.

Fur is reached by ferry from Branden (on the northernmost part of Salling). There is a coach route from Skive to Debel. The inn Fuur Gæstehjem serves an excellent fried eel.

Area 11. Vendsyssel

1: Albæk Hede: About 12 km south of Sæby by A10 to Dybvad, then south-east to Albæk. The moor, which is a protected area, lies between Albæk and Vorså villages, north of Faurholt farm. On the moor are vast stretches of Iron Age fields and to the west on the Holtbjerg hills are several groups of Bronze Age barrows placed along the Stone Age coast line.

2: Blakshøj: 1 km south of Gerum parish church which about 8 km south-west of Frederikshavn. The large mound, Blakshøj, covers a fine passage grave with an oval chamber built of fifteen uprights and five solid capstones. The chamber was excavated in the 1880's; only a few flint axes and some potsherds were found.

3: Donbæk is a small village only a few km south-west of Frederikshavn. 1 km south-west of the village is a protected area with sixty-two small barrows on a sloping hillside. About twenty barrows were excavated during the years 1907-9; most of the smaller ones covered cremation graves from the Early Germanic Iron Age (fifth to sixth century A.D.). The finds—urns, combs, and modest personal ornaments—are in the National Museum. The larger barrows contained burials from the Roman Iron Age.

4: Dronninglund Storskov: A pretty wood only a few km north of Dronninglund. In the eastern half of the wood, just east of the road to Flauenskjold, are two large, magnificent barrows and two smaller ones. The group is named 'Knaghøje' and it is placed on top of the highest point above sea level (135 m) in Vendsyssel. In the south-western part of the wood, near the road, is a fine long barrow about 80 m long and a few hundred meters to the east is another long barrow of about 40 m length. The area south of the wood has many fine groups of barrows.

75

Plate 9. One of the small Donbæk barrows, No. 19, dating from the Germanic Iron Age, photographed during the excavation (Area 11, No. 3)

5: Filholm is a farm about 7 km north-west of Brønderslev (from Brønderslev to Tolstrup church and then 3 km westwards), where stands a large Late Neolithic stone cist built of five uprights and three capstones. The cist was excavated in 1938; the finds were two flint daggers, some amber beads and a bone awl, which are in the National Museum.

6: Galgehøj (i.e. the gallows-hill): From Hjørring by A11 to Vittrup, then southwards by the road to Børglum church. West of the road is a fine Bronze Age barrow.

7: Grønhøj: About 8 km south-east of Fjerritslev, about 0.5 km east of Bejstrup village is a large dolmen with two chambers. Further east towards Haverslev village are four barrows one of which is a fine long barrow named Hødeshøj.

8: Gunderupgård is a farm about 6 km south-east of Fjerritslev, 0.5 km south-west of Skræm station. Near the farm are two megalithic burials and a Bronze Age barrow. The northern passage grave has a chamber of 12.5 m length and remains of two passages; near these are two smaller chambers. The southern passage grave has a central and an extra chamber which was excavated in 1855 by the National Museum; several flint implements and amber beads were found. Just east of Skræm station is a fine long dolmen, 70 m long, with two chambers. The dolmen was excavated by the National Museum in 1878; several amber beads and a flint axe were found.

9: Hammer bakker (hills): Just north of Ålborg between A11 and A14, heather grown and with small plantations. In this area are several groups of Bronze Age barrows and Neolithic long dolmens and also many deep-cut tracks of prehistoric lanes.

10: Hjorthøj: is a beautiful Bronze Age barrow just south of Dronninglund storskov, west of the road to Flauenskjold, with a fine view of the surrounding scenery from the hill-top which rises 89 m above sea level.

11: Hjørring: At Stationsvej is a Bronze Age barrow with three burials. The barrow was excavated in 1938 and the finds—a bronze dagger, a bronze sword and an urn (from a late Bronze Age burial) are in Hjørring Museum. At Hjørring cemetery are eight stone cists from the Roman Iron Age; they were excavated in 1933 and yielded excellent finds—pottery, glass, and iron implements—which are in Hjørring Museum.

12: Horne cemetery: About 12 km north of Hjørring, west of the church tower, is a Late Neolithic stone cist of which five uprights and one capstone are left, on the capstone are several cup-marks. Two clay vessels, a flint dagger, and two flint arrow-heads from the cist are in the National Museum.

13: Hoven: 13 km north-east of Hjørring, 0.5 km east of Mygdal church, is a long dolmen with twenty-two peristaliths and in the centre the remains of a capstone.

14: Hune church: About 20 km west of Brønderslev by the road to Blokhus. In the church is a rune-stone with the following inscription, 'Hove, Thorkil, and Thorbjørn erected this stone to their father, Runulf the resourceful'.

15: Hvissehøj: at Alsbjerg, a small village about 14 km south-east of Fjerritslev. Hvissehøj is a most unusual passage grave, the only one of its kind in Denmark. The passage was demolished in the 1850's, but the chambers are left—not less than three of them one leading out of another. The first chamber is 8 m long, the second 4.8 m, and the third 2 m long. All three chambers were excavated by the National Museum in 1915. The chambers had been in use during the Middle and Late Neolithic periods. Also Bronze Age burials were found. The finds are in the National Museum.

Among the hills around Alsbjerg are many fine groups of barrows.

16: Hørbylund: About 10 km west of Sæby between Gundestrup village school and Hørbylund is a long dolmen just west of the road. The dolmen has a rectangular chamber built of five uprights. West of Gundestrup village school is a small dolmen built of five uprights and a threshold facing south. The capstones are reconstructed.

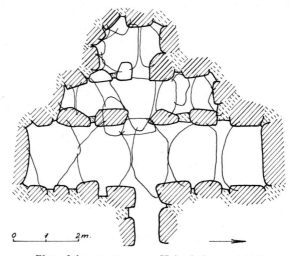

4. Plan of the passage grave, Hvissehøj, near Alsbjerg
(Area 11, No. 15)

17: Jetsmark church: On A11 about 22 km south-west of Brønderslev. In the porch of the parish church is a rune-stone which was found at Pandrup, a nearby village; the inscription reads, 'Hove erected this stone to his brothers Thorlak and Ride'.

18: Kabelhede: 20 km east of Hjørring by A11 to Sindal, then north and west to Mosbjerg and Vejen (or by train to Tolne). Kablehede is south of the road, here is a dolmen chamber built of three uprights and one capstone. The finds from the chamber, eight flint axes and amber beads, are in the National Museum. North of the road is a fine group of Bronze Age barrows named Ellevehøje (i.e. the eleven barrows).

19: Lindholm høje is at the western outskirts of Nørre Sundby, just north of Ålborg across the Limfjord. The site is covered with about seven hundred burials and traces of several houses, excavated during the years 1952–9 and afterwards restored so that it is now our most impressive prehistoric site. The oldest burials date from the sixth century A.D., mostly cremation burials, now marked as small mounds. The later burials are inhumation graves, those from the eighth and ninth centuries A.D. were marked with various stone enclosures such as squares, triangles, ovals or circles. From the Viking period date the ship-formed burials (enclosing a cremation patch), but about thirty inhumation graves date from the latest Viking Age; they are marked with small mounds and are mostly found in the south-eastern part of the site.

The town was placed north of the hill; several houses, a road built of planks, and six wells were found. During the centuries the burial-ground was devastated by sand-drifts and during the later Viking Age became completely buried so that the town crept southwards across the sand dunes, more than twenty houses were excavated here. Both rectangular and oval houses were found, the latter being of the same type as the Fyrkat and Trelleborg houses (see Area 7, No. 7 and Area 18, No. 36). At the southernmost parts several fields were excavated, also covered by sand dunes, they date from the latest years of the town's existence, about 1100.

Visitors must remember that the site never looked like what it does now. The incessant sand-drifts throughout the centuries gradually buried the hill and covered the burials of past years.

The finds from Lindholm are in the Ålborg Museum.

Plate 10. Lindholm Høje seen from the air. The postholes of the houses are filled in with concrete (Area 11, No. 19)

20: **Margrethelund plantation:** 3 km west of Dronninglund, between the plantation and the road to Torup is a dolmen the chamber of which has five uprights; the capstone is not preserved. North of the dolmen are a few Bronze Age barrows. In the southern part of the plantation on a hillside called Lundebjerg are several barrows.

21: **Rampen:** About 17 km west of Sæby, by A10 to Dybvad, then westwards to Hejselt Manor. West of the Manor, near a small stream, is the beautiful long dolmen called Rampen, not less than 125 m long (one of our longest long dolmens); at the eastern end is a well-preserved square chamber with capstone and an entrance facing south. Four thin-butted flint axes and an amber bead were found in the chamber; the finds are in the National Museum. Near this dolmen is another rather ruined long dolmen and a long barrow of about 90 m length. On the eastern side of the Skæve–Torshøj road is a well-preserved Bronze Age barrow named Tohøj.

22: **Ravsten:** South-east of Fjerritslev between Bejstrup church and Søndervang (see also site No. 7) is a fine dolmen chamber built of four uprights and one capstone.

23: **Rødland hede:** About 10 km north-east of Fjerritslev by A11 then north-east to Fosdal plantation. Rødland hede is a stretch of moorland south of the road from Hjortdal to Øster Svenstrup. On the moor are several well-preserved prehistoric fields framed by 0.5 m high earthen dykes. Most of the fields are rectangular from 30 × 40 m up to more than 150 m.

24: **Skavange:** 18 km west of Sæby, just north of Torslev parish church is a rectangular dolmen chamber which contained a collared flask, a thin-butted flint axe, and several amber beads. The finds are in Hjørring Museum. Between the passage uprights is a small stone cist from the late Bronze Age.

25: **Stenbakken:** 10 km south-east of Sæby by A10 to Dybvad then northwards to Vester Haven Manor. Between the Manor and the small wood, Kvistskov, is a dolmen built of five uprights and one capstone. Just north of the dolmen are two groups of barrows, to the south a group of four, further north another group of three barrows of which one is a long barrow 46 m in length.

26: **Stenhave:** 6 km west of Frederikshavn by A11. Stenhave is a farm about 1.5 km south of the road; just outside the farm is a fine long dolmen, 28 m long, with a ruined chamber and thirteen large peristaliths.

27: Stenhøj: (the same route from Hjørring as site No. 18), north of Tolne church is a long dolmen of 35 m length with eighteen peristaliths and a ruined chamber. South of the church are several groups of well-preserved Bronze Age barrows.

28: Stenstuen at Gerum: 7 km south-west of Frederikshavn is a fine long dolmen of 70 m length with more than fifty peristaliths some of which are overturned, and in the eastern end the remains of a ruined chamber.

29: Store Ingsbjerg: 2 km north-west of Sæby, north of the small wood Sæbygård skov is a barrow covering a rather ruined passage grave, about 7 m long.

30: Sudergårde: 6 km west of Dronninglund at the outskirts of a small plantation is a group of six barrows among which is a well-preserved long barrow of 93 m length. South of the plantation are two barrows named 'Gallows hills'.

31: Tornby: 10 km north of Hjørring by the Hirtshals road is a fine dolmen chamber built of three uprights. South of Tornby church is a long dolmen of 51 m length with two rather ruined chambers. 2 km north-east of Tornby is a hill, Tornby bjerg, crowned with a Bronze Age barrow. The view from this site is truly magnificent.

32: Torstendal: 17 km east of Brønderslev by the road leading through Klæstrup–Jerslev–Hellum–Skæve. Between Hellum and Brønden east of Pajhede skov is a long dolmen, 44 m long with nine peristaliths and a rectangular chamber built of four uprights and one capstone. Along the road south of the wood are several Bronze Age barrows.

33: Vangsgårde: 3–4 km west of Frederikshavn, just west of Flade church is a fine group of Bronze Age barrows crowning the hills, with an excellent view of the surrounding countryside. 16 km west of the church is a mound covering one of the finest dolmens of the district; the chamber is built of five uprights and one capstone. About 0.5 km further west is a circle of eleven stones with a flat stone in the centre. The date of this enclosure is uncertain.

The principal museum of this area is Vendsyssel's Historiske Museum, Hjørring. The excellent prehistoric collections are especially rich in Celtic and Roman Iron Age pottery; the Vendsyssel pottery from these periods is of outstanding quality. Open during the summer season every day from 10–12 noon and from 1–5 p.m., and during the winter season every day from 1–3 p.m.

Try Museum (a small town 4 km south-west of Dronninglund) has a good local collection mainly representing finds from the eastern part of Vendsyssel.

Hjørring is the capital of Vendsyssel and well suited for visits to the sites Nos. 6, 11–13, 18, 27 and 31 (sites Nos. 18 and 27 can just as easily be approached from Frederikshavn).

The coach station is opposite the railway station. The Tourist Information Office is at Rådhusstræde 9.

Hotels: Phønix, Jernbanegade; Skandia, Springvandspladsen; Afholdshotellet, Østergade 9 (not licensed); Corner, Banegårdspladsen; Landmandshotellet, Nørregade 2; Martin's hotel, Jernbanegade 19.

Fjerritslev is well situated for visits to the sites Nos. 7, 8, 15, 22 and 26. About Fjerritslev see Area 9, Thy.

Ålborg is a good starting point for the sites Nos. 9, 19 and 33. About Ålborg see Area 8, Himmerland.

Dronninglund is well situated for visits to the sites Nos. 4, 10, 20 and 30. Good coach and train connections. Dronninglund is a station on the Ålborg–Sæby and Dronninglund–Ørsø–Aså lines.

Hotel: Dronninglund hotel.

Frederikshavn is well suited for visits to the sites Nos. 2, 3, 18, 26–8. The coach station is at Kirkepladsen (church square). The Tourist Information Office is at 'The Tourist Terminal', Trafikhavnen.

Hotels: Hoffman's hotel, Danmarksgade 62; Bech's hotel, Jernbanegade 4; Højskolehotellet, Jernbanegade 7; Motel Hoffman, Sæbyvej 12; Turisthotellet, Margrethevej 5–7.

Brønderslev is well suited for visits to the sites Nos. 5, 14, 17 and 32. The coach station is at Jernbanegade; Brønderslev is a railway station on the Ålborg–Frederikshavn line.

Hotels: Phønix, Bredgade 9; Central-hotellet, Nørregade 2.

Sæby is well suited for sites Nos. 1, 16, 21, 24, 25 and 29. The coach station is at Krystaltorvet. The town is a railway station on the Ålborg–Sæby line.

Hotels: Viking, Frederikshavnsvej; Harmonien, Vestergade; Dania, Vestergade.

THE ISLANDS
Area 12. Funen (Fyn)

1: Alleskov (also called Kohave): In this pretty little wood about 2 km east of Fåborg on the road to Holstenshus are several fine megalithic monuments: A long dolmen with thirty-one peristaliths and a chamber covered with a gigantic capstone; very near this burial is another long dolmen, about 33 m long, with about seventy peristaliths; the dolmen has a single chamber and the passage faces south. 25 m east of this dolmen is a small barrow covering a Late Neolithic stone cist. 25 m from this barrow is a fine dolmen 47 m long, framed by twenty-seven large peristaliths. The polygonal chamber was excavated in 1954; the finds date from the Middle Neolithic period and are in Fyns Stifts-museum, Odense.

2: Ellested: From Nyborg by A8 to Ørbæk and then 3 km to the west by A9 from Odense to Ringe and about 10 km to the east. On the northern side of the road is a pentagonal dolmen chamber. Not all the peristaliths are preserved.

3: Esterhøj or **Hesthøj:** 14 km north of Kerteminde and 1 km east of Martofte village is a fine passage grave covered by a mound of up to 5 m height, the chamber is almost 7 m long.

4: Glavendrup: 15 km north-west of Odense by the Odense–Bogense road to Bladstrup, then 3 km west to Glavendrup. A large ship-formed burial with a rune-stone placed as the prow (cf. Bække, Area 4, No. 1). The inscription on the stone is the longest rune-stone text known in Denmark: 'Ragnhild erected this stone to Alle the Pale (?), priest of the sanctuary, the housecarls' noble chieftain. Alle's sons made these memorials to their father and his wife to her husband, but Sote engraved the runes to his master. May Thor consecrate these runes. A Ræte (probably troll) the man who dare ruin this stone or use it as a memorial for another (man)'. The ship-formed burial was excavated and restored in 1958, it was found to frame a small cemetery of Viking Age date with cremation patches.

5: Grisemosehøj, near Ferritslev, 17 km south-east of Odense on the Ørbæk road. North of Ferritslev village, 300 m from the road is a fine long dolmen, 28 m long, with 33 peristaliths and a chamber, 2 m long, with three uprights and one capstone and an entrance facing north-east.

6: Gåsestenen, near Emmelev. 15 km north-west of Odense, by the Bogense road to Bladstrup, then north-east through Hjadstrup and Brandsby to Emmelev. About 1 km N.N.E. of the village is a small passage grave, the chamber is 3 m long and built of seven uprights and two capstones. The chamber was excavated in 1954; it contained finds from the Middle and Late Neolithic periods. The finds are in Fyns Stiftsmuseum.

7: Horneland is the small peninsula in the south-western part of Funen, west of Fåborg. Several prehistoric monuments are placed in this area; among the most noteworthy are some megalithic tombs near Bjerne village. About 200 m east of Knoldsborg farm is a small mound covering the remains of a passage grave, one of the capstones has several cup-marks. A fine passage grave is placed about 100 m N.N.W. of the farm, it is about 4.5 m long and is built of eight uprights and three capstones. About 100 m N.N.E. of the farm is a dolmen chamber of rectangular shape, built of three uprights, a large lintel, and one capstone.

8: Jorløse: About 15 km north-west of Fåborg by the Svanninge–Håstrup–Jorløse road. About 100 m south of the road and 2 km south-east of Jorløse parish church is one of the finest round dolmens of Funen. The mound is 16 m broad and bordered with twenty-one large peristaliths; in the centre is a rectangular chamber covered by one gigantic capstone in which several cup-marks can be seen.

9: The Ladby ship-burial: About 4 km west of Kerteminde near Nymarksgården farm (road signs indicate 'Ladbyskibet'). The only Danish ship-burial from the Viking period, excavated in 1935. Only traces of the ship were left, or rather, its imprint in the soil (just like the Sutton Hoo ship). The excavation has been covered with a concrete vault covered with turf so that the impression is much like what it was when the original mound covered the burial. The ship was 22 m long, built of five or six planks at either side. The burial chamber was aft of the mast but it was, unfortunately, plundered. In the prow were found the skeletons of eleven horses and four dogs. In the showcases are several copies of the finds, the originals are in the National Museum. The Ladby ship mound is open daily in the summer season from 10 a.m.–6 p.m., and October–March from 10 a.m.–3 p.m.

10: Lindeskov: is on the Ørbæk–Ringe road (see the sites Nos. 2 and 5); 2 km west of Ørbæk and a few hundred meters north of the road is the longest Danish long dolmen, 168 m long with 126 peristaliths and at the northern end a small chamber without capstone. 200 m further west on the Ørbæk–Ringe road a country lane leads to a grove called Lindeskov Hestehave, in which are several monuments: a mound covering a stone cist built of six uprights and two capstones, two long dolmens which are, unfortunately, rather ruined, and a round dolmen surrounded by twenty-one peristaliths.

11: Munkebo: 7 km west of Kerteminde, 0.5 km north of Munkebo parish church are two mounds each covering a passage grave. One is 5 m long, built of eleven uprights with a passage facing east, the other is 3 m long and built of eight uprights. Both passage graves were excavated in 1911; the finds—from the Middle Neolithic Period—are in the National Museum.

12: Mårhøj: (or Moreshøj) 1 km north of Esterhøj (No. 3) just north of Martofte on the road to Snave village is a gigantic mound covering Funen's largest passage grave. The passage is 7 m long, the chamber measures 10 m and is built of eighteen uprights and seven large capstones.

13: Pipstorn wood: 5 km east of Fåborg between the road and the railway. Beginning from the western part we find first a beautiful long dolmen, 34 m long, with 53 large peristaliths and three chambers. 200 m further east are three long dolmens placed very near each other; there are six chambers of which only one has no capstone. In the central part of the wood is a large Bronze Age barrow and in the eastern part of the wood, near the railway line, is a group of fifteen Bronze Age barrows.

14: Ringshøj: From Odense to Årslev by A9, then east to the farm Ringstedgård; about 350 m north-east of the farm is Funen's largest barrow, probably of Bronze Age date, it is 9 m high and almost 50 m in diameter.

15: Rolfshøj: 15 km south-east of Odense by the Ørbæk road to Rolsted, 0.9 km north-west of Rolsted church by the inn Rolighedskroen is a long dolmen, 17 m long and 10 m broad. There are two chambers, the western one has several cup-marks on the capstone.

16: Skamby: 15 km north-west of Odense by the Bogense road, then west to Skamby. About 600 m north-east of Skamby church on the road to Bare Brøndstrup village is a small passage grave, the chamber is 3 m long and built of nine uprights; of the passage six stones are left. The chamber was excavated in 1931, the finds—from the Middle Neolithic Period—are in the National Museum.

17: Svenskerhøj: Just west of Nyborg, about 300 m south of A1 by the 27 km stone is an imposing Bronze Age barrow, 5 m high and 26 m in diameter, one of the very few Bronze Age barrows on Funen which has escaped total demolition.

The principal museum is Fyns Stiftsmuseum, Jernbanegade, Odense. The museum has excellent collections from the prehistory of Funen, especially the Roman Iron Age is well represented. Open daily from 10 a.m.–5 p.m., Sundays 10–12 noon and 2–4 p.m. (1st April to 30th September), and 10 a.m.–3 p.m., Sundays 10–12 noon and 2–4 p.m. (1st October to 31st March).

Funen is such a small island that any prehistoric site may be reached from the capital, Odense, within a few hours by train, coach or car. If, however, smaller towns should be preferred those will be listed below.

Odense is well suited for the sites Nos. 2, 4–6, 10, 14–17 (sites Nos. 2 and 10 can just as easily be approached from Svendborg). The coach station is at Vestre Stationsvej 5; about thirty different routes are run. The Touristr Infomation Office is at the Town Hall, the Vestergade entrance.

Hotels: Grand, Jernbanegade 18; Motel Odense, Hunderupgade 2; Park Hotel, Ålykkegade 2; Axelhus, Hans Tausensgade 19; Missionshotellet Ansgar, Ø. Stationsvej 32; Ny Missionshotel, Ø. Stationsvej 24; Ansgarhus Motel, Kirkegårdsalle 17–19.

Svendborg (sites Nos. 2 and 10) is a pretty seafaring town with many old houses. The Tourist Information Office is at Klosterpladsen 9. Hotels: Svendborg, Voldgade; Klostergården, Klosterpladsen 4; Ny Missionshotel, Brogade 2–4; Royal, Toldbodvej 5.

Svendborg is also well suited for visits to the Tåsinge sites (see Area 13).

Kerteminde is well suited for visits to the sites Nos. 3, 9, 11 and 12. The coach station is at the railway station. The Tourist Information Office is at Langegade 5. Hotel: Tornøes hotel.

Fåborg is a good starting point to the sites Nos. 1, 7, 8 and 13. The coach station is at the railway station (train connection Nyborg–Mommark–Sønderborg), the Tourist Information Office is at Torvet 5. Hotels: Rasmussens hotel, Torvet 12; Hotel Horseløkke, Svendborgvej; Hotel Teglgården, Svendborgvej 68.

Area 13. The Islands South of Funen:
Lyø, Ærø and Tåsinge

Lyø is reached by ferry from Fåborg. On this tiny island were once about eighteen megalithic tombs of which only six are preserved. The prettiest of these is the dolmen chamber, Klokkestenen, not far from the west coast, 1.5 km from Lyø town. The chamber is built of six uprights and one large capstone. Halfway to Klokkestenen is a small dolmen chamber, about 100 m north of the road.

East of Lyø town, about 1 km from the church, is a dolmen chamber built of six uprights and one capstone. The chamber was excavated and restored in 1946; only a few flint blades were found.

Ærø is reached from Funen by ferry from Svendborg to Ærøskøbing or from Langeland by ferry from Rudkøbing to Marstal. There is a coach route Marstal–Ærøskøbing–Søby.

The island was densely populated during the Neolithic Period. We know of about 160 prehistoric monuments but only thirteen are preserved and protected. Not less than about ninety of these monuments were situated within Rise parish and of these only eight remain. 200 m north-west of Rise church is a fine long dolmen, 54 m long, with two chambers of which only one has a capstone. At the north-western end is a round barrow about 2 m high and 20 m in diameter. By Rise rectory is a long dolmen called Tingstedet, and just south of the farm called Risemark is another long dolmen with many peristaliths; the capstone of the chamber is broken in two. About 1.5 km further east is another long dolmen, the chamber of which has two capstones. Near Lindsbjerg, south of the road to Marstal are two long dolmens, the one to the west has two rectangular chambers and the other has two small passage grave chambers. At Søby, about 15 km west of Ærøskøbing is a rectangular dolmen chamber with an overturned capstone.

Tåsinge is reached by bridge from Svendborg (the distance is about 1 km) or from Langeland by the bridge from Rudkøbing across Siø.

1: **Bregninge:** In the rectory garden is a large, flat-topped barrow, 4 m high and 28 m in diameter. The date is either Bronze Age or Iron Age.

2: Ingershøj: is 1.5 km south of the ferry harbour, just east of the road to Bregninge, a fine Bronze Age barrow crowning a hill-top, the mound is 7 m high and 41 m in diameter.

3: Taersminde: About 2 km south-east of Bregninge, just south of Taersminde farm is a mound covering a passage grave; the rather ruined chamber is oval, 9 m long and 2.3 m broad.

Marstal is the largest town on Ærø and one of the prettiest seafarer's towns in Denmark. The Tourist Information Office is at Kirkestræde 7. Hotels: Ærø. Hotel Marstal, Dronningestræde.

Ærøskøbing is an almost undisturbed idyll of seventeenth and eighteenth century town-planning. The Tourist Information Office is at Smedegade 12. Hotels: Harmonien, Brogade; Ærøhus, Vestergade.

Tåsinge is most conveniently placed for a visit from Svendborg (see Area 12, Funen).

Area 14. Langeland

1: Bjergbygård: 5 km north of Rudkøbing, turn west at the 5 km stone. Between the road and a small grove is a long barrow with two passage grave chambers. The northern chamber has cup-marks on one of the capstones.

2: Egeløkke: 20 km north of Rudkøbing, just west of Bøstrup, is Egeløkke Manor; in its grounds is a small mound covering two small passage graves. The mound was excavated in 1953 and it was apparent that the chamber had been in use throughout the Middle Neolithic Period. The finds are in Langelands Museum, Rudkøbing.

3: Hulbjerg: 27 km south of Rudkøbing, not far from Bagenkop, just east of Søgård farm is a mound covering a passage grave. The chamber was excavated in 1960. The finds date from the end of the Middle Neolithic and the Late Neolithic Periods. The finds are in Langelands Museum.

4: Konabbe skov: 11 km south of Rudkøbing to Lindelse and then west through Hennetved to the hill Ellensbjerg in the small wood Konabbe skov. At the foot of the hill is the only ship-formed burial known from Langeland. It probably dates from the Viking Age.

5: Kong Humbles grav (King Humble's grave): 13 km south of Rudkøbing, just east of the road is one of our finest long dolmens and the largest known from Langeland, 55 m long, with seventy-seven large peristaliths. There is only one chamber with a short passage and one enormous capstone.

6: Kædeby: 13 km south of Rudkøbing. A fine dolmen chamber built of large peristaliths and with a gigantic capstone on the top of which are about thirty cup-marks.

7: Løkkeby is about 7 km north-east of Rudkøbing. In the grounds of Petersgård farm is a beautiful long dolmen with one chamber.

8: Myrebjerg: 2 km north of Bagenkop, east of the road by Magleby Nor. At the foot of the hill, Myrebjerg, is a long dolmen containing a passage grave with an oval chamber and a short passage with lintels. The monument was excavated in 1877 and 1950; during the excavation it was observed that the long dolmen was built on an artificial platform of stone and clay. The finds date from the Middle Neolithic and Late Neolithic Periods, a late Bronze Age urn was also found in the chamber. The finds are in Langelands Museum.

9: Nygård: About 28 km north of Rudkøbing is the small wood Bræmlevænge; in its south-eastern part are several small and low round barrows dating from the Late Bronze Age.

10: Pæregård: 10 km north of Rudkøbing. A long dolmen with large peristaliths and three chambers each with a short passage. The dolmen was excavated in 1951. In one of the chambers was found the skeleton of a young girl placed on top of the bones of at least nineteen persons. The chamber had been in use throughout the Middle Neolithic Period. The finds are in Langelands Museum.

11: Skovtofte: 17 km north of Rudkøbing, turn west to Kelletofte north of Tranekær; in the small wood south of the village is a passage grave with a large chamber and a short passage placed in a long dolmen. Excavated 1948–9. The floor was covered with stone slabs; here several vessels were found dating from the later part of the Middle Neolithic Period. The older burials had been removed and were found outside the peristaliths together with sherds of ritual vessels. The finds are in Langelands Museum.

12: Snage skov: 10 km north of Rudkøbing to Frellesvig huse, then west to Snage skov. On a hill-top in the wood is the long dolmen Ringelshøj, bordered with more than a hundred peristaliths; the chambers are more or less in ruins.

13: Statene: Is a tiny village 6 km south of Rudkøbing. In a ploughed down barrow are two large pear-shaped megalithic tombs.

14: **Stengade skov** is about 10 km north-east of Rudkøbing. Near the coast is a group of four small barrows from the Late Bronze Age.

15: **Tryggelev:** 16 km south of Rudkøbing is a small long dolmen excavated and restored in 1958 so that it now looks like what all dolmens must have looked like when they were new. The mound is bordered by peristaliths with dry-walling between them. The chamber has a short passage. The burials dated from the later part of the Middle Neolithic Period and the Late Neolithic Period. A Late Bronze Age urn burial was found in the mound. The finds are in Langelands Museum.

16: **Tved skov:** About 1.5 km south of Tranekær is a small wood east of the road to Stengade; in its south-western part is a small long barrow with a double passage grave, a rare occurence in this part of the country as double passage graves most often occur in North Sealand (Areas 16 and 17) and North Jutland (Areas 8 and 11).

Langeland is reached from Zealand by ferry Korsør-Lohals or from Lolland by ferry Nakskov–Spodsbjerg.

Rudkøbing is the largest town. Here is the excellent museum, Langelands Museum, with a very fine prehistoric collection especially from the Middle Neolithic dwelling sites Klintebakken, Troldebjerg, Blandebjerg and Lindø, and remarkably good finds of Viking Age burials (especially the Stengade cemetery). The museum is open from 10 a.m.–4 p.m. (June–August) and 2–4 p.m. except Mondays rest of the year. The museum is closed on Christmas Day and New Year's Day.

The coach station runs several routes on the island. The Tourist Information Office is at Østergade 8. Hotels: Langeland, Torvet 2; Rudkøbing, Havnegade 2; Skandinavien, Brogade 13.

Area 15. Samsø

1: **Besser:** South-east of Besser village is the high coast cliff and only a few meters from the cliff-edge is a Late Neolithic stone cist of which only the uprights remain; the capstones are not preserved.

2: **Brattingsborg:** North-west of Brattingsborg Manor is a group of four barrows, Hyldehøje, all four originally covering a passage grave. Now only two chambers remain.

3: **Rævebakkerne** (i.e. the fox's hills): At Sælvig Bay north of Toftebjerg village and east of the road is a group of six Bronze Age barrows.

4: **Stenstuen:** North of the small village Alstrup, east of Toftebjerg, is a well-preserved dolmen built of four uprights and one capstone.

5: **Toftebjerg:** West of Toftebjerg and east of the road to Nordby is a long dolmen called Niels Halds høj.

6: **Ørby** is a small village in the southern part of Samsø. Just east of the village and north of the road is a passage grave, not very well preserved. One of the fallen capstones has many cup-marks.

Samsø is reached from Zealand by ferry from Kalundborg to Kolby Kås and from Jutland by ferry from Århus.

Samsø Museum is at Tranebjerg; the museum has a small prehistoric collection of finds from the island. The museum is open during the summer season every day from 9–11 a.m. and from 2–5 p.m.

Tranebjerg is the largest town. Coaches run to Nordby–Onsbjerg–Kolby Kås, Toftebjerg–Kolby Kås, and Ballen–Kolby Kås–Onsbjerg.

Hotel: Flinck's hotel.

Area 16. North-West Zealand (Sjælland)

1: **Asnæs** is the peninsula south of Kalundborg Fjord. In the small wood, Forskoven, there are forty-five barrows; in the western wood, Vestskoven, there are twenty-seven. The larger barrows are undoubtedly from the Early Bronze Age, the smaller ones from the Late Bronze Age.

2: **Dutterhøje:** About 20 km south of Nykøbing by the Holbæk road to Keldstrup, then south-west by the road to Asnæs village. Dutterhøje is a beautiful group of Bronze Age barrows about 2 km south-west of Keldstrup. 2 km north-west of Dutterhøje (near Høve) is another group of five barrows and a fine long dolmen, Kæmpegraven, of 60 m length. Further west, just outside Høve on the road to Fårevejle, is a fine group of barrows, Esterhøj is the largest with a beautiful view of the sea and the surrounding scenery.

Plate 11. The group of Bronze Age barrows, 'Dutterhøje' at Asnæs (Area 16, No. 2)

3: Frenderup: About 15 km north of Holbæk, just south of Frenderup village, is a long dolmen with about thirty peristaliths and one, un-covered, chamber. Just by Frenderupgård farm is a beautiful round dolmen with a hexagonal chamber, a large capstone and a broad passage; the peristaliths are of considerable size.

4: Grevinge skov is a small wood 2 km north of Frenderup. Beside the road through Østrup to the wood is a fine round dolmen with a pentagonal chamber, a lintel, and a large capstone. In the centre of the wood is a round dolmen the chamber of which is built of five uprights and one rather defective capstone; the passage is built of two pairs of uprights. In the eastern outskirts of the wood is the long dolmen 'Hamlet's tomb' (there are, by the way, several 'Hamlet's tombs' in Denmark); it is 39 m long and has sixty peristaliths, the chamber has no capstone. In the western part of the wood is a round dolmen with a narrow chamber built of three uprights, one capstone and a lintel.

5: Gørlev church: About 20 km south of Kalundborg on the Slagelse road. In the porch of the church is a rune-stone which was found underneath the stairway in the southern porch. The inscription reads, 'Thjod erected this stone to Odinkar' followed by the runic alphabet (the 'fupark') 'Use the grave well. I wrote the runes well. Gunne, Armund. . . .'

6: Herrestrup: About 15 km north of Holbæk on the road to Nykøbing is Herrestrup village, 1 km to the south-west is the round dolmen, Dilhøj, with a hexagonal chamber and one gigantic cap ne with Bronze Age rock engravings of ships and sun symbols.

7: Højby: 6 km west of Nykøbing. South of the village near the railway is a fine Bronze Age barrow called Brynshøj. About 1 km west of the village near the farm Sekshøjgård is a round dolmen with a pentagonal chamber and one gigantic capstone covered with cup-marks. 0.5 km north-east of Sekshøjgård is a long dolmen called Toftebjerg; a short passage leads to a hexagonal chamber covered by a large capstone. Between Højby and the Nykøbing–Holbæk road is a fine group of six Bronze Age barrows.

8: Nyrup: About 5 km west of Nykøbing. In this village are two megalithic monuments, Birkehøj, with an 11 m long chamber and a passage covered by six capstones, and Skingshøj with a hexagonal chamber built of five uprights and a passage built of two uprights, on the capstone are a few cup-marks.

9: Reerslev: About 25 km south-east of Kalundborg by the Slagelse road to Sæby and then about 5 km east to Reerslev. 1 km west of Reerslev is a group of five bauta stones from the Viking Period. East of the village are six dolmens: four round and two long dolmens, among which is a long dolmen not less than 100 m long (one of the longest in the country); of the four chambers three are preserved.

10: Refsnæs (also spelled Røsnæs) is the peninsula north of Kalundborg Fjord. Raklev is a village about 2 km west of Kalundborg. Three megalithic monuments are grouped round the village, to the east is a round dolmen with four uprights and a capstone, in the centre is a long dolmen with three chambers; one of the capstones has several cup-marks. West of the village is are constructed dolmen chamber in a private garden. The chamber comes from a now demolished long dolmen. On the road to Nyrup (not the same as the Nyrup village described as No. 8) are more megalithic monuments; first a long dolmen, rather ruined, with no chambers preserved, then a passage grave chamber (in a private garden) without capstones, and near this a dolmen built of five uprights, capstone, and a lintel. About 200 m further west is a double passage grave without capstones. The chambers were excavated in the 1870's and the finds—potsherds and flint axes from the later part of the Middle Neolithic Period—are in the National Museum.

About 1 km north of Raklev, near Ellede, are two bauta stones called 'Standfast and his brother'.

On the road to Refsnæs (Røsnæs) village are two dolmen chambers built of five uprights each and a bauta stone on top of a mound. About 2 km east of the village on the road to Ågerup is a round dolmen built of four uprights, a lintel, and a capstone, and north of Ågerup not far from the coast is a long dolmen, 30 m long with fine peristaliths and a rather ruined chamber.

11: Ruds Vedby: About 25 km south-east of Kalundborg (see No. 9). West of the village are six megalithic monuments placed between the road and the railway: first a pretty long dolmen with three chambers, then a long dolmen with a narrow chamber without capstone, then a third long dolmen with a rectangular chamber and towards the western end a small passage grave. Near this long dolmen is a round dolmen and in the same field three long dolmens and one round dolmen. South of this group is a long dolmen, the chamber of which has no capstone. West of Ruds Vedby are two dolmen chambers, one built of three uprights, lintel and capstone, the other rather in ruins.

12: Rørby is 5 km south-east of Kalundborg. Just north of the village on the road to Kærby is Nordenhøj or Loddenhøj, a double passage grave which was excavated in 1885. The finds were axes, amber beads and much pottery, which are in the National Museum. About 1 km north-east of Nordenhøj is Olshøj, a mound covering a double passage grave. South of Nordenhøj near the road to Værslev is the double passage grave Hyldehøj which was excavated in 1887.The finds are the richest hitherto found in a Danish passage grave: skeletons of more than 100 persons, many flint axes, chisels, arrow-heads, amber beads, and clay vessels, mostly from a later part of the Middle Neolithic Period. The finds are in the National Museum. Nearer to Værslev are two passage graves, one on either side of the road; the one on the north-west has three chambers and the one on the south-east has one chamber which has not been excavated.

13: Stenstrup: About 10 km west of Nykøbing. 1 km west of Stenstrup is a mound covering a monumental double passage grave bearing the name 'Troldestuen' (i.e. the troll's chambers). Two passages of 6 m length lead to a chamber each, both chambers are 7 m long and 2 m broad. The chambers were excavated in 1909; most of the finds were flint daggers and vessels from the Late Neolithic Period. The finds are in the National Museum.

14: Ubby: About 12 km south-east of Kalundborg is an area rich in megalithic monuments. South of Nygård farm near the Rørby–Svallerup road is a dolmen chamber built of five uprights and one capstone. North of Nygård at a place called Dysselodden (i.e. the dolmen acre) are three passage graves of which two are very well preserved. Further east, on the Rørby-Ubby road, is a Bronze Age barrow which was excavated in 1884; the burials were inhumation graves from the Early Bronze Age and urn burials from the Late Bronze Age. The finds are in the National Museum. Just outside Ubby is the fine double passage grave, Korshøj (in a private garden), which was excavated in 1843 (the northern chamber) and 1939 (the southern chamber). The finds from the southern chamber were axes, arrow-heads, and some very fine clay vessels from the Middle Neolithic Period. The finds are in the National Museum.

15: **Vejrhøj** is only a few km west of Fårevejle—where James Hepburn, Earl of Bothwell, is buried; his mummified body can be seen in the crypt—a flat-topped Bronze Age barrow crowns the hill-top Vejrhøj (121 m above sea level). The barrow is 40 m in diameter and 8 m high. The view from this hill is the most magnificent to be found on the Danish islands.

The principal museum within the area of North-West Zealand is Holbæk Museum, Klosterstræde, Holbæk. The museum is open daily in May–October from 2–5 p.m. and October–May, Tuesdays, Thursdays and Sundays from 2–5 p.m.

Kalundborg Museum at Lindegården (opposite the church) has a good prehistoric collection especially from the famous Mesolithic site at Mullerup. The museum is open during the winter season from 10–12 noon and 2–4 p.m. During the summer season from 10–12 noon and from 2–6 p.m.

Holbæk is a good starting point for the sites Nos. 3, 4, 6, 13 and 15. Holbæk is a railway station on the Copenhagen–Kalundborg and Holbæk–Nykøbing lines. The coach station is at Jernbanegade 2, the Tourist Information Office at Nygade 1.

Hotels: Strandparken, Kalundborgvej 58; Jernhotellerbane, Jern-banevej 1; Isefjord, Ahlgade 4; Missionshotellet, Nygade 12.

Kalundborg is well situated for visits to the sites Nos. 1, 5, 10–12 and 14. Trains run Copenhagen–Kalundborg and Slagelse–Kalundborg. Ferry connections to Århus, Samsø, and Juelsminde. The coach station is by the railway station. The Tourist Information Office is at Kordil-gade 26.

Hotels: Grand Hotel, Skibbrogade 1; Jernbanehotellet, Skibbrogade 2; Ole Lunds Gård, Kordilgade 1–3; Sømandshjem and Missionshotel, Nygade 12; Postgården, Kordilgade 6.

Nykøbing is well situated for visits to the sites Nos. 2, 7 and 8. The coach station is at Jernbanevej. The Tourist Information Office is at Algade 41.

Hotels: Odsherred, Algade; Phønix, Algade; Hotel 'der Vest', Algade.
Slagelse is a good starting point for the sites Nos. 9 and 10. About Slagelse see also Area 18, South Zealand.

Area 17. North-East Zealand (Sjælland) and Copenhagen

1: Copenhagen: Even the metropolis can boast of a few prehistoric monuments although none in the heart of the town. In the northern suburbs Hellerup, Gentofte and Charlottenlund several monuments are to be found. Just north of Hellerup church between the roads Margrethevej and Aurehøjvej is the fine Bronze Age barrow, Aurehøj (in a private garden). At Gentofte there is Elhøj at the corner of Højgårdsalle and Ewaldsbakken, and Baunehøj at the corner of Vangedevej and Skolebakken. At Vældegårdsvej are the two barrows called Brødrehøje. In Charlottenlund Skov are about ten small barrows. Nearer to the centre of the town is the park Bellahøjparken with four barrows. In the suburb Rødovre is the large Bronze Age barrow, Valhøj, in Henrik Cavlings alle. In the north-western suburb Gladsakse is a small dolmen chamber just south of Gladsakse church near the Inner Ring Road and the imposing Bronze Age barrow, Garhøj, in a small park at Holmevej.

2: Dråby: The northern part of Hornsherred is very rich in prehistoric monuments. About 5 km from Frederikssund is Jægerspris Castle; 0.5 km north of the castle is Julianehøj, a passage grave, the exterior of which was much altered in the eighteenth century when it was excavated by Prince Frederik. The chamber is 8 m long, built of fifteen uprights and five capstones. The passage still remains unexcavated. The rune-stone on top of the mound is from Norway. In the park is another passage grave, excavated in 1744 by Prince Frederik (later King Frederik V). The chamber is built of eight uprights and three capstones; the passage is much restored. The Latin inscription commemorates the royal excavation. A few km north, in the wood Nordskoven, are several groups of larger and smaller Bronze Age barrows, and west of the wood, between the road and the coast south of Hjortegårde farm, are first (from north to south) a mound covering two unexcavated passage graves, then two mounds covering a passage grave each. The southernmost of these was excavated in the 1880's. The chamber is covered by three capstones, then two dolmen chambers;

both have the capstone preserved. South of these megaliths is a group of eleven barrows.

3: Dæmpegård: In the wood Tokkekøb Hegn between Hørsholm and Hillerød, about 7 km from Hillerød is Dæmpegård farm (turn north by the 10 km stone) with a beautiful long dolmen surrounded by twenty-two peristaliths and with two covered chambers.

4: Græse: About 6 km north-east of Frederikssund near the road from Græse to Hørup is one of the longest passage graves in Denmark; the chamber is 12 m long and built of twenty-seven uprights, the passage is built of seven uprights and two capstones. The floor of the chamber is covered with stone slabs. The passage grave was excavated in 1924 and yielded rich finds of axes, daggers, spear heads, amber beads and pottery vessels. The finds are in the National Museum.

5: Grønnessegård: About 8 km west of Frederiksværk and about 0.5 south of the Hundested–Frederiksværk road is Grønnessegård farm with the beautiful dolmen chamber called Carlsstenen built of five uprights and one capstone.

6: Gundsølille: About 10 km north of Roskilde by the Himmelev road. Between the villages of St Valby and Gundsølille is a mound covering two passage graves which were excavated in 1876. The finds —axes, amber beads, flint chisels, arrow-heads, and pottery—are in the National Museum.

7: Gundsømagle is about 5 km north of Gundsølille. In this village is a long dolmen Hødyssen, surrounded by large peristaliths, with one chamber built of four uprights and one gigantic capstone decorated with about twenty-five cup-marks. Of the other chamber only a few uprights remain.

8: Hedehusene: About 7 km east of Roskilde (25 km from Copenhagen) by A1. In the garden in front of the church is a rune-stone bearing the inscription, 'Hornborne's stone, Svide's scion'.

9: Kyndeløse: About 20 km north-west of Roskilde by A4 and then north through Lyndby and Kirke–Hyllinge; Kyndeløse is west of Kirke–Hyllinge. 1 km south of Kyndeløse village is Møllehøj, a mound

Plate 12. Group of Bronze Age barrows at Bakkebjerg near Rågeleje (Area 17, No. 12)

covering a double passage grave with oval chambers and two passages. The chambers were excavated in 1937. The finds date partly from the latter part of the Middle Neolithic Period (flint axes, amber beads, excellent pottery) and partly from the Late Neolithic Period (flint daggers). The finds are in the National Museum.

10: Lejre: About 7 km west of Roskilde between A1 and A4. A ship-formed burial 29 m long, fifteen and twelve stones remain at each side. The 'ship' was excavated in the 1950's and was found to frame a Viking Age cemetery (tenth century) of more than twenty inhumation graves. Near the ship-formed burial is the barrow Hesthøj and the more or less ploughed-out Grydehøj which was excavated in 1958. The mound covered a large cremation patch from the Later Iron Age.

11: Rungsted: 22 km north of Copenhagen by Strandvejen (the Coast Road). Just north of the harbour is a large Bronze Age barrow, the exterior of which is slightly altered (a winding flight of steps leads to the top where there is a memorial stone to the poet Johannes Ewald). Behind this barrow is a group of three well-preserved Bronze Age barrows (in a private garden).

12: Rågeleje: 22 km north-east of Frederiksværk, to Helsinge and then north through Valby to Bakkebjerg (or from Helsingør by Græsted-Blistrup to Bakkebjerg). At Bakkebjerg is a group of eight large Bronze Age barrows, one of the finest groups in Zealand. 3 km north-east of

Bakkebjerg is the double passage grave Ølshøj (near Ølshøjgård farm) covered by a large mound. The southern chamber is 3.60 m long and built of eight uprights, the passage is 6 m long and built of five pairs of uprights and three capstones. The northern chamber is 2.80 m long and built of eight uprights and three capstones. In the southern part of the mound is a Late Neolithic stone cist which was found and excavated in 1961; two skeletons and one flint dagger were found.

13: Skodsborg: 15 km north of Copenhagen by Strandvejen or by train (the coast line) to Skodsborg. South of the station between the railway and the Coast Road is a large mound with two Late Neolithic stone cists. The skeletons are reconstructed in concrete. About 700 m south of the stone cists, just west of the railway line are two Bronze Age barrows which were excavated in 1863 by the archaeologically minded King Frederik VII. In the western barrow was a stone cist containing a sword, a palstave, and a belt hook, in the eastern mound several urns were found.

14: Stasevang: is a tiny wood about 6 km north-west of Hørsholm, 2 km north of the Hørsholm–Hillerød road (see No. 3). In the southeastern corner are two dolmens, a round dolmen and a long dolmen with two chambers. In the centre of the wood is a fine dolmen with three chambers, and in the northern part is a long dolmen with two rectangular chambers without capstones.

15: Tibirke Ellemose: About 12 km north-east of Frederikssund in the peat-bog, Tibirke Ellemose, between Tibirke hills and Horsebjerg is a 150 m long stretch of a road, or ford, dating from the Celtic Iron Age. The road is 3 m broad and built of stones within a frame of kerbstones; parallel to the road is a path of a single row of stones.

16: Udlejre is a small village about 10 km south of Frederikssund on the Roskilde road. About 1 km north of the road to Ølstykke are two long dolmens, Dødningerne (i.e. the dead men). One is rather well-preserved, with two chambers, of the other only fragments are left. Just west of the road to Ølstykke is a beautiful passage grave, Møllehøj, which was found and excavated in 1797. The chamber is almost 7 m long, built of fifteen uprights and four capstones. The passage is built of ten uprights and four capstones.

17: **Valby Hegn** is a pretty little wood just north of Helsinge (see No. 12, Rågeleje), from south to north along the path in the western half of the wood are the following monuments to be seen: a long dolmen with two chambers, of which only one has the capstone preserved; a long dolmen the chamber of which is a small passage grave covered with two capstones; a long dolmen with one chamber, the capstone of which is decorated with several cup-marks; a small long dolmen with two chambers; two long dolmens placed near each other, both have many well-preserved peristaliths and three covered chambers; a long dolmen with many peristaliths preserved and two uncovered chambers.

18: **Øm**: 5 km south-west of Roskilde by A1 to Øm, through the village and then westwards towards Lejre. Øm passage grave is one of the finest and best preserved in the country; an imposing mound covers the chamber which is 7 m long, built of fifteen uprights and four capstones. The passage is built of seven pairs of uprights, one lintel, and one capstone. The stone fence surrounding the mound is of nineteenth-century date.

The principal museum of this area is—of course—the National Museum in Copenhagen, or rather, not only of this area, it is the Prehistoric Museum of the whole country. The Prehistoric Department covers the whole country; in its archives are registered descriptions and maps concerning all the several thousand prehistoric monuments known to us. The prehistoric collections are open every day except Tuesdays from 11 a.m.–3 p.m. (winter season) and 10 a.m.–4 p.m. (summer season). Office hours Monday–Friday 12–4 p.m.

Frederikssund is well situated for visits to the sites Nos. 2, 4, 9, 16 and 17 (site No. 9 can just as well be reached from Roskilde). The coach station is at Torvet. Train connection to Copenhagen. Hotels: Isefjord, Havnegade 19; The Ferry Inn, 'Bilidt' Færgevej 100.

Roskilde is well situated for visits to the sites Nos. 6–10 and 17. The coach station is opposite the railway station. Excellent train connections Copenhagen–Korsør, Næstved, Gedser, Rødby ferry, and Kalundborg. The Tourist Information Office is at Stændertorvet. Hotels: Prinsen, Algade 31; BP Motel on A1 by the 31 km stone; Hotel Roar, Algade 12; Motel Risø near Himmelev, 1 km from Roskilde.

Frederiksværk is well situated for visits to the sites Nos. 5 and 15. The coach station is at the railway station. Train connections to Hillerød and Hundested. Tourist Information may be obtained from the bookseller's, Nørregade 24. Hotels: Frederiksværk, Torvet; Grand Hotel, Nørregade 10.

There are also numerous hotels at the many seaside resorts on the coast from Copenhagen to Helsingør and Hundested, but these are almost always booked up months in advance of the summer season.

Area 18. South Zealand (Sjælland)

1: Alsted: About 10 km south-west of Ringsted, south of A1. In the parish church is a rune-stone with the following inscription, 'Eskil erected these stones to Østen and his brother Flir, Østen's son, Adelmærke'. 1.5 km east of the church is the long dolmen Halkensten-dyssen with three rectangular chambers and well-preserved peristaliths.

2: Ammendrup: 15 km north-east of Vordingborg, on the road Vordinborg–Mern–Præstø. 1 km west of Ammendrup village is the fine passage grave 'Rishøj'. The chamber measures 6.5 × 2 m; built of fourteen uprights and five capstones, the passage is 7 m long.

3: Bildsø: About 10 km north-west of Slagelse. 2 km west of Bildsø near Knudsrødgård farm is a long dolmen with a rectangular chamber, and a few kilometers further east, between Bildsø and Kirke Stillinge, is the round dolmen Grimskærdyssen with many well-preserved peristaliths and cup-marks on one of the uprights. 1 km west of Grimes-kærdyssen, near Kærrebygård farm, is a well-preserved long dolmen with three chambers and many peristaliths.

4: Boeslunde: 12 km south of Slagelse. 1 km north-west of Boeslunde is a fine dolmen chamber built of seven uprights and one capstone. 2 km west of Boeslunde, south of the road to Korsør, is a group of four Bronze Age barrows. In the north-eastern corner of the small wood Klarskov is a large mound with a stone cist—one of the only three stone cists which are preserved in South Zealand.

5: Borreby: 4 km south of Skelskør, west of the road to Magleby, is a passage grave (the mound was dug away in 1858); the chamber is built of ten uprights and two capstones, the passage of five pairs of uprights and two capstones. J. J. Worsaae excavated the chamber in 1859. Several artefacts from the Middle Neolithic and Late Neolithic Periods were found and also skeletons of about sixty persons mostly of a brachycephalic type which differs from all other known skeletal material of Neolithic date.

6: Bregentved park and home wood: (open only Sundays and Wednesdays) 25 km south-east of Ringsted. Small groups of Bronze Age barrows, twenty-two barrows in all.

7: Broby Vesterskov: About 10 km south of Sorø, north of the lake Tystrup sø. In the wood Broby Vesterskov are several prehistoric monuments: from north to south there is first a round dolmen with peristaliths, the chamber built of three uprights and one lintel; then a long dolmen with a ruined chamber; a long dolmen with several peristaliths, the chamber built of five uprights and one capstone; then a long dolmen with peristaliths but without a mound, the capstone of the chamber decorated with cup-marks. Further south are two round dolmens and one long dolmen and a group of ten Bronze Age barrows.

South of the river Suså is a small wood, Enemærket, with a group of ten small Bronze Age barrows and a ruined dolmen with about seventy cup-marks in the capstone.

8: Broskov: 4 km north-west of Præstø. A prehistoric stone-built road dating from the Celtic Iron Age, built as a ford across the low-lying, water-logged meadow. On top of the very well-built Iron Age road is the mediaeval ford built of much smaller stones. In the nearby woods are several deep-cut trackways leading to the ford.

9: Fjenneslev: Halfway between Sorø and Ringsted, just south of A1. By the road branching off from A10 (by the 67.4 km stone) to Fjenneslev is the mound Baunehøj with a passage grave without capstones. In Fjenneslev cemetery is a rune-stone which tells that 'Sasser erected the stone and built the bridge'. The stone probably came from the bridge Sasserbro (i.e. Sasser's bridge) which spans the river Tuelå 4 km south-west of Fjenneslev.

10: Fuglebjerg is a village about 20 km north-east of Skelskør by the road through Eggeslevmagle and Ting Jelling. 1 km south-west of Fuglebjerg is a mound covering a passage grave; the rectangular chamber is covered by four capstones, the passage is uncovered. 2 km west of Fuglebjerg by the road from Sneslev to Kirkeskov is a small passage grave chamber.

11: Glumsø: 12 km south-west of Ringsted. In the small wood, Glumsø Østerskov, east of the town are ten more or less ruined round dolmens and long dolmens. East of the wood just by the road between Vinderup and Herluflille is a fine round dolmen with peristaliths and a chamber built of six uprights and one large capstone. In a field just north of Herluflille is a long dolmen with peristaliths; of one chamber two uprights and a capstone are visible.

12: Grøfte: is a small village about 5 km south-east of Sorø. Just south of the railway are two long dolmens, one has peristaliths and a chamber built of four uprights, the other is also surrounded by peristaliths and has two chambers each built of three uprights and one capstone. A third long dolmen which was ploughed out during the nineteenth century was excavated in 1946, two chambers were found which had been completely covered by the mound; they contained pottery of Early Neolithic date, skeletons and a flint halberd. The finds are in the National Museum.

13: Gunderslevlille: is a village 15 km south of Sorø on the Sorø–Næstved road. Between the road from the 15 km stone to Gunderslev-lille there are, from north to south, the following monuments: a round dolmen the chamber of which is built of six uprights and one capstone; a long dolmen surrounded by peristaliths, with a chamber built of four uprights and one capstone and in the southern end a group of long dolmens and a passage grave covered by a mound. A few km further north, where the Glumsø road leads off to the road to Sorø, is a long dolmen with two rather ruined chambers, a round dolmen with a pentagonal chamber and a mound, Storkebjerg, which covers a passage grave; five capstones can be seen on the top of the mound. 2 km further north, just east of the Sorø road, at Atterup village, is a well-preserved long dolmen with three chambers; the mound is surrounded by peristaliths.

14: Hårlev: 14 km south of Køge on the road to Fakse. In the cemetery is a flat-topped barrow, probably of Late Iron Age date. An old tradition says that the imposing rune-stone called the Tryggevælde stone, which is now in the National Museum, once stood on top of the barrow. The inscription which is closely related to the Glavendrup inscription (see Area 12, Funen, No. 4) reads, 'Ragnhild, Ulf's sister, erected this stone and this ship-formed burial to her husband Gunulv, son of Nærve, Few are born (who are) better than he. A troll the man who ruins this stone or takes it away from here'.

Plate 13. The Kirke Stillinge dolmen chamber with Bronze Age rock engravings (Area 18, No. 17)

15: **Kanehøj:** is an imposing Bronze Age barrow 3 km north-east of Skelskør on the Eggeslevmagle road (see No. 10). In the nineteenth century the barrow was a place of execution, and the poet Hans Andersen, then a pupil in Slagelse Grammar School, witnessed an execution here in the 1820's which he has described in his autobiography.

16: **Kellerød:** 7 km south of Sorø by the Skelskør road. About 1 km east of the road is a long dolmen, 125 m long (the longest long dolmen east of the Belt), surrounded by low peristaliths. The chamber is in the northern end; it was excavated in 1933 and was found to serve as a burial for a single person, a sixty-year-old man, buried with a flint knife and a clay flask of Early Neolithic date. The skull had been trepanned, but the man did not long survive the operation. The finds are in the National Museum. About 16 km further south, just north of the road to Vinstrup, is a fine dolmen chamber and a long dolmen with two ruined chambers.

17: **Kirke Stillinge:** 9 km north-west of Slagelse, 1–2 km south of the village on the road to the coast is a group of megalithic monuments; about 200 m north of Kelstrup is a fine long dolmen with cup-marks on the capstone of the southern chamber, and 300 m to the south-west is a dolmen chamber called Ugledysse (i.e. The Owl's Dolmen), built

of five uprights, one capstone, and a lintel. A few hundred meters
south-west of Kirke Stillinge is the rather ruined long dolmen,
Breddysse, which is well worth seeing as one of the capstones is decorated with Bronze Age rock engravings of two ships and sun symbols.
A few km to the south-west just on the coast is a fine long dolmen with
three chambers surrounded by peristaliths; the western end of the
mound has slid into the sea. Nearby is a small passage grave covered
by a mound and a long dolmen with two chambers. On the Slagelse
road (south of the 5 km stone) is a row of six fine Bronze Age barrows
placed along an ancient trackway.

18: Knudshoved Odde: is the long, narrow peninsula west of Vordingborg. South of the road to Orehoved Manor and about 1 km south of
the house is Troldhøj which covers a fine passage grave; the chamber is
10 m long and has six capstones. In Oreby skov are (taken from east
to west) first a large mound covering a passage grave, then a fine Bronze
Age barrow, and a long dolmen with a well-preserved chamber and
peristaliths. North of the wood by the road through Knudsby village
is a ruined mound with two chambers which were excavated in 1937.
the few finds date from the later part of the Middle Neolithic period.
Further west along the only road on the peninsula is a fine passage
grave with a covered passage, and 1.5 km further west an imposing long
dolmen with peristaliths and two well-preserved chambers, then another
long dolmen with a rectangular chamber. In the small wood, Knuds-
skov, is a mound covering a passage grave. Past the narrow passage
called Draget the scenery is of unequalled beauty. It can only be
explored on foot (all vehicles must be left at Knudskovgård farm).
It is a true Bronze Age landscape with scattered oaks and hawthorns
where are a stone half-circle and three parallel rows of stones, about
25 m long; the date of these monuments are uncertain.

19: Krømlinge: A small village about 10 km east of Næstved by the
road through Rønnebæk, Nestelsø and Brandslev. Halfway between
Brandelev and Krømlinge in the south-west corner of the wood
Brandelevholme is a beautiful long dolmen, 18 m long, with two
chambers and surrounded by peristaliths; a row of stones are placed
across the mound. In the village is a long dolmen, not very well preserved, but the covered chamber is intact, and a round dolmen covered
by a large capstone.

20: Landsgrav: A village 4 km west of Slagelse, north of A1. In the village is the beautiful long dolmen called 'The King's Dolmen' or 'The Slagelse Dolmen'; it is 57 m long and surrounded by eighty enormous peristaliths. Bavnehøj is a fine Bronze Age barrow lying close to 'The Twin Barrows' and 'Hellig Anders høj' (the Holy Anders' Mound). The crucifix on the barrow is rooted in the legend about the pious pilgrim, Anders, who fell asleep on the shore of the Holy Land and woke up on the barrow outside Slagelse. This group of barrows is all that is left of twenty-two prehistoric monuments built near the ancient trackway mentioned under No. 17, Kirke Stillinge.

21: Magleby skov: About 15 km south-east of Køge on the east coast of Stevns. In the wood are two dolmens and several groups of Bronze Age barrows, the largest of these consists of twenty-one mounds. Further south the wood changes its name to Gjorslev Bøgeskov; near the lake Møllesøen (the mill-pond) are two groups of twenty-seven and twenty-two rather small barrows which probably date from the Late Bronze Age.

22: Maglehøj: About 15 km south of Køge by the road to Strøby then southwards to Valløby; 2 km south of Valløby on the road to Hellested is the imposing passage grave Maglehøj. The mound is 4 m high and 15 m in diameter. The chamber is not of imposing size, 6 m × 2 m, but well built of fifteen uprights and four capstones; the passage is 4 m long, built of six pairs of uprights and three capstones. The chamber was opened in 1823 and several flint and stone implements were found which were given to the National Museum.

23: Næsbyholm skov: The wood south of Broby Vesterskov (No. 7) east of the lake Tystrup Sø is extremely rich in monuments—not less than 118 Bronze Age barrows and a few megalithic tombs. In the northern part of the wood is a ruined dolmen, the now overturned capstone is decorated with about seventy cup-marks. In the southern part of the wood are a long dolmen and a mound covering a passage grave, the capstone can be seen on top of the mound. South of the wood, on the road to Bavelse church, are two long dolmens of which the southernmost has two chambers.

24: Ortved: A village 7 km north-east of Ringsted by A1. In a private garden by the 55 km stone is a Late Neolithic stone cist which was originally covered by a mound. The cist was excavated in 1940; it contained fragments of three or four skeletons and a flint dagger.

25: Sandby: 9 km south of Ringsted. In the cemetery of the parish church is a fragmentary rune-stone on which only part of the inscription is preserved, 'Eskil erected this stone to his brother Tue . . . and . . .'.

26: Skovhuse skov: A small wood about 8 km east of Vordingborg. In the centre of the wood is a long dolmen, 22 m long, and in its eastern outskirts is a group of seven monuments, a long barrow 25 m long and 2 m high, five barrows of varying size and a bauta stone, which is 1.5 m high. 2 km south of Skovhuse wood is Langebæk village (just south of the road Vordingborg–Kalvehave). In a field near the village is a group of three passage graves, one of these has a chamber of 3 m length, built of eight uprights and two capstones. The other two passage graves have never been opened or excavated.

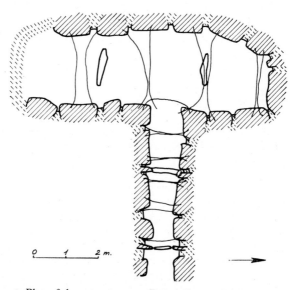

0   1   2 m.

5. Plan of the passage grave, Rævehøj, near Slotsbjergby
(Area 18, No. 27)

27: Slotsbjergby: 3 km south of Slagelse by the Skelskør road are two gigantic barrows, Hashøj and "The Gallow's Hill', both of which command a lovely view of the surrounding scenery. The Gallow's Hill was excavated by the National Museum in the 1940's. In the top were found the foundation posts of the gibbet which stood here until the first half of the nineteenth century. Several skeletons of hanged and beheaded persons were found. The centre of the mound is of Bronze Age date; during the later Iron Age the mound was enlarged to its present site, but no burials from this period were found.

1.5 km south-west of Slotsbjergby (turn west at the 5 km stone) is the passage grave, Rævehøj, which was excavated by the National Museum in 1914. The mound which is about 40 m in diameter reached its present size during the Bronze Age. The passage is long and well built; the chamber is rather ruined as some of the uprights were removed during the Late Neolithic period to give access to the chamber. About a hundred skeletons were found during the excavation; most of the finds date from the Late Neolithic period.

28: Sneslev Kalvehave: 9 km from Ringsted by the road to Haslev are on either side of the road a small passage grave and a dolmen chamber built of five uprights, on the capstone are two cup-marks. 1 km east of these megaliths is the imposing mound, Lådenhøj, which covers a double passage grave. The chamber is 16 m long and built of thirty uprights; two uprights divide the chamber into two parts each of which has its own passage.

29: Sorø Sønderskov: The wood east and south of Sorø. 1 km east of Sorø and 300 m south of A1 is a fine long dolmen, 30 m long, surrounded by large peristaliths. 1.5 km further south is the mound Svinebakke in which is a megalithic chamber.

30: Stensby skov is a small wood on the south coast about 10 km east of Vordingborg. In this wood are (from west to east) a mound covering a passage grave; a long dolmen of 17 m length with a covered chamber; two closely placed long dolmens, 16 m and 17 m long, of which several peristaliths are preserved, but the chambers are uncovered; a mound covering a passage grave; and a long dolmen, 60 m long surrounded by peristaliths, of which no chambers are visible.

31: Store Bøgeskov: 12 km north-west of Ringsted by the road through Gyrstinge. In the wood on the western side of the lake Gyrstinge Sø there is, in the south-western part, a most impressive long dolmen surrounded by large peristaliths and with two rather ruined chambers; across the western end is a row of stones.

32: Strandegårds Dyrehave: 5 km south of Fakse Ladeplads. From Vordingborg (or Køge) by A2 to Tappernøje, then east through Nørre Smidstrup to Roholte and Store Elmue. In the wood near the coast is a beautiful group of four Bronze Age barrows and the remains of what was once a ship-formed burial probably of the Viking Age. West of the wood in Store Elmue village is a passage grave the chamber of which is 11 m long.

33: Stubberup skov: About 5 km north of Fakse Ladeplads (about approach see site No. 32). In the north-eastern part of the wood is a beautiful long dolmen, 50 m long, with two covered chambers and many well-preserved peristaliths.

34: Stubby: 5 km north of Vordingborg by the road to Næstved. 1 km west of the village is Milehøj, which covers a fine passage grave with a rectangular chamber, 12.5 m long and 2.5 m broad. The chamber was excavated and restored by the National Museum in 1917, but as the chamber had previously been plundered no finds are known.

35: Svinø: 15 km north-west of Vordingborg. In the small cluster of farms, Svinøøster, is the mound Månehøj, covering a double passage grave which was excavated by the National Museum in 1908. The finds comprise about 300 objects, mostly pottery, from the Middle Neolithic Period. The chambers are only divided by a single upright; two long, narrow passages lead to the chambers.

36: Trelleborg: 5 km west of Slagelse. This Viking fortress was the first of its kind to be found in Denmark. The fortress is divided into two parts: first the outer fortress consisting of a half-circular wall protecting thirteen houses the axes of which radiate from the centre of the circular wall. The circular wall has four gates which were covered by planks when the fortress was in use. Inside the wall stood sixteen houses placed four and four in squares (just like Fyrkat), they measure 29.5 m (i.e. 100 Roman feet), the houses in the outer fortress measure ninety Roman feet. The mathematical precision with which this site is constructed is quite amazing and commands respect for the Viking kings, Sven Tveskæg and Canute, during whose lifetime fortresses of this type flourished. The finds from Trelleborg date the fortress to about A.D. 950–1050. The excavation and restoration of this gigantic complex took place during the years 1934–40. Outside the circular wall is a life-size reconstruction of a Trelleborg house.

37: Udby: 8 km north of Vordingborg by A2. 1 km west of Udby village is a fine long dolmen, 16 m long. Many peristaliths are still standing, and the chamber is covered by a large capstone. About 0.5 km south of the dolmen is a large Bronze Age barrow, Trudshøj; its original height was about 10 m. The mound was excavated by the National Museum in 1895, and was found to contain a stone cist 4 m long in which stood the now famous 'Skallerup wheeled cauldron' filled with burned bones. The wheeled cauldron is of Central European (urn-field culture) or maybe North Italian origin.

38: Vielsted: North of Store Bøgeskov (see No. 31) and 1 km north of the wood, just east of the road to Vielsted village is the best preserved round dolmen to be found in the whole country; it is of truly magnificent size, surrounded by large peristaliths and both chamber and passage are covered by one gigantic capstone.

39: Ørslev: 5 km north-west of Vordingborg, 1 km south of Ørslev village is the long dolmen called 'The cemetery of Rynkebjerg'. The mound is 34 m long and surrounded by many peristaliths; of the three chambers only ruins are left. Near the dolmen is a small passage grave chamber, 3 m long, built of six uprights and one capstone.

Vordingborg Museum is the museum of South Zealand, it is placed near the ruins of Vordingborg Castle and has good local collections both of prehistoric and later finds. Open daily during the summer season from 9–12 noon and from 1–5 p.m. During the winter season till 4 p.m. Closed on Sundays.

Næstved Museum is at Helligåndshuset, Ringstedgade 4. The museum has only a small prehistoric collection. Open daily from 2–4 p.m.

Stevns Museum is at Højerup Cliff near Store Hedinge, not far from the abandoned parish church of Højerup. The museum has a good small collection of local finds, especially of Stone Age flint implements. Open daily from Easter until 1st October from 2–4 p.m.

The South Zealand area is so small that it can easily be covered from Copenhagen or from one of the many smaller towns, such as Ringsted, Sorø, Vordingborg, etc. Below are listed the towns most conveniently suited for visits to the various sites.

Ringsted for the sites Nos. 1, 6, 7, 9, 11, 24, 25, 28, 31 and 38 (site No. 7 can just as well be approached from Sorø). The town has train connections on the line Copenhagen–Korsør and to Næstved. The coach station is at the railway station. Tourist Information can be obtained at the bookseller's, St. Hansgade 9 and at hotel Casino. Hotels: Casino, Torvet; Postgården, Nørregade 2.

Sorø is the county town of South-west Zealand and a pretty idyll in the heart of the beech-woods, well situated for the sites Nos. 7, 12, 13, 16, 23. Railway connection Copenhagen–Korsør. The coach station is at Storgade 8. The Tourist Information Office is at Torvet (during the summer season), and at Absalonsgade 34 (winter season). Hotels: Postgården, Storgade 27; Kong Frederik, Storgade 10; Parnas, opposite the town across the lake.

Slagelse for the sites Nos. 3, 4, 17, 20, 27 and 36. Railway connections Copenhagen–Korsør, to Kalundborg and to Næstved. The coach station is opposite the railway station. The Tourist Information Office at Fisketorvet. Hotels: Postgården, Gammel Torv 1; Ny Missionshotel, Banegårdspladsen.

Skelskør for sites Nos. 5, 10 and 15. The coach station is at the railway station. Tourist information may be obtained at the bookseller's, Algade 27. Hotels: Postgården, Strandgade 4–6; Centralhotellet, Østergade 8.

Vordingborg for the sites Nos. 2, 8, 18, 19, 26, 30, 32–35, 37 and 39. Railway connection Copenhagen–Næstved–Gedser/Rødby Ferry. The coach station is at the railway station. The Tourist Information Office is at Algade 86. Hotels: Prins Jørgen, Algade 1; Boulevard-hotellet, Boulevarden 12.

Køge for the sites Nos. 14, 21 and 22 (and maybe also Nos. 32 and 33). Railway connections to Copenhagen–Næstved and Køge–Hårlev–Fakse Ladeplads/Rødvig. The coach station is at Torvet and the Tourist Information Office at Stationspladsen 5. Hotels: Hvide Hus, Strandvej; Centralhotellet, Vestergade 3; Hafnia, Jernbanegade 14; Motel Søvilla, Ølsemagle near Køge.

Area 19. Lolland

1: Birket: About 17 km north-west of Maribo. South of the village and north-east of the church is Bavnehøj, a Bronze Age barrow which is the largest on Lolland, it is 7 m high and placed on a hill-top. South-west of Bavnehøj are three Bronze Age barrows, a fourth can be found in the cemetery where it is used as a foundation for the wooden mediaeval belfry. 1 km north-east of Birket is the large mound 6 m high, Glentehøj, which covers one of the best-preserved Danish passage graves. The chamber is 9 m long and of almost pear-shaped ground-plan, a characteristic feature of Lolland's passage graves; the passage is 5 m long and built of four pairs of uprights. Just south-east of Glentehøj are three well-preserved Bronze Age barrows.

2: Flintinge Byskov: is a small wood 7 km east of Sakskøbing, south of A7 to Nykøbing. In the centre of the wood is a beautiful passage grave (the mound is not preserved), the chamber is more than 7 m long and the passage measures 3.75 m. The chamber was excavated in 1879; many skeletons were found and several objects from the later part of the Middle Neolithic Period such as axes, chisels, daggers, amber beads, and potsherds. The finds are in the National Museum.

Near the passage grave, to the south, is a long dolmen with a ruined chamber, and north-west of the passage grave is a small long dolmen with twenty-five peristaliths and two chambers.

3: Frejlev Skov: About 7 km north of Nysted, east of the Nysted–Nykøbing road is a small stretch of wood, facing the coast of Guldborg-sund, it is 4 km long and 1.5 km broad—not an imposing size—but within this modest area are four round dolmens, five passage graves, nine long dolmens, and more than a hundred Bronze Age barrows!

In the eastern part of the wood are two small passage graves, of which the chambers are about 6 m long; both graves have been excavated by the National Museum. The finds of axes, chisels, amber beads, and pottery vessels date from the Middle Neolithic period. Between the

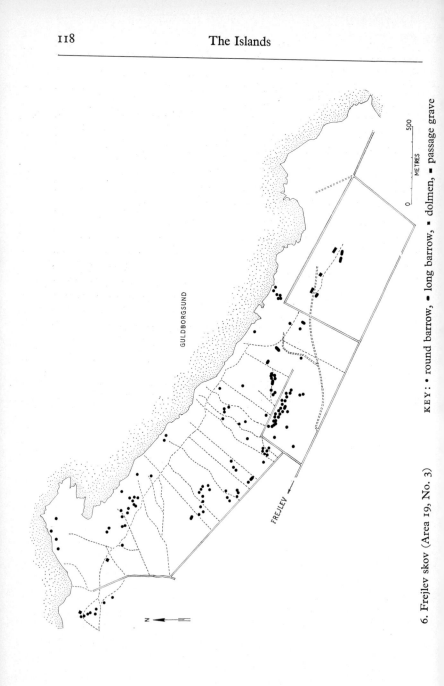

6. Frejlev skov (Area 19, No. 3)

KEY: • round barrow, ▪ long barrow, ▪ dolmen, ▪ passage grave

Plate 14. One of the many passage graves in Frejlev skov seen from the entrance to the chamber (Area 19, No. 3)

passage graves is a fine round dolmen, one of the best preserved on the island. A little further west is an imposing long dolmen called 'Kong Grønnes Høj'. Most of the Bronze Age barrows are rather small; they date from the Late Bronze Age.

4: Guldborg Storskov: 5–10 km north-east of Sakskøbing is a small wood, rich in prehistoric monuments. From the village Soesmarke a road leads through the wood to the south-west; along this road, just inside the wood, is a large group of small barrows from the Late Bronze Age. West of the road, near to the barrows, is a long dolmen, 21 m long, with two chambers the capstones of which are covered with cup-marks. In the south-western part of the wood is the passage grave, Splitov's Høj, the chamber of which is 9 m long. In the northern part, near the path from Soesmarke to Kallø Skovby, is a small round dolmen surrounded by fifteen peristaliths; the chamber is built of four uprights.

5: Idalund: About 10 km east of Sakskøbing, by A7 to the 10 km stone, then northwards through Krungerup to Idalund Manor. West of the Krungerup road is a long dolmen, 50 m long, surrounded by fifty-six peristaliths and with one chamber. South-west of Idalund, in the wood, is a passage grave the chamber of which is 8 m long, and the passage 7 m long. The chamber is covered by five capstones. About 500 m east of the Manor is a group of forty-two small barrows dating from the Late Bronze Age.

6: Kong Svends Høj (i.e. King Svend's mound): 15 km north-east of Nakskov between Svinsbjerg and Pederstrup Manor is the passage grave, Kong Svends Høj, which has the county's longest chamber: 12.30 m long and built of not less than twenty-seven uprights, the seven capstones are of truly magnificent size. The passage grave has been known since 1770 when Count Reventlov of Pederstrup excavated the chamber (with little result), the 6 m long passage escaped notice until 1942 (when the monument was restored) maybe because it faces west: passage grave corridors almost always face east.

7: The Maribo Lakes: About 10 km east of Maribo by the road to Engestofte Manor and then southwards to Bøgeskov (i.e. the Beech Wood) and Hejrede, along this road, just north of the lake, is a group of nine Bronze Age barrows and south of the lake is another group of forty-five barrows. In the tiny wood south of Hejrede lake, is a group of forty-three small barrows of Late Bronze Age date placed very close together. West of these woods is the wood Storskoven, just north of the road through this wood is a group of twenty-five barrows and about as many scattered over a larger area. All these small barrows, from 0.5 to 2 m in height, cover urn burials from the Late Bronze Age.

8: Nagelsti: From Nykøbing by the Maribo road about 5 km, then eastward to Priorskov Manor. Just after this turn is a fine dolmen chamber in a field near the road. A short distance further east is another dolmen chamber, without capstone. North and north-west of Priorskov Manor are two long dolmens one of which is surrounded by forty peristaliths. From Priorskov turn to the north to Nagelsti village. West of the village is a beautiful long dolmen, 60 m long, and surrounded by seventy-four peristaliths.

9: Orebygård Manor: 5 km north-west of Sakskøbing. About 1 km north-east of the Manor is a stone cist which is about 3 m long and 2 m broad, and built of eight uprights; only two capstones remain; a passage 2.5 m long leads off from the south-western end of the chamber. The burial was excavated in 1877; the finds of axes and pottery vessels (three skeletons were also found) belong to the East Danish Battle-Axe Culture. The stone cist is a most unusual kind of burial in this part of the country.

10: Radsted: 4 km east of Sakskøbing by A7. South of the road, just west of Radsted village, is one of the longest dolmens on the island, 80 m long and 9 m broad surrounded by 119 peristaliths. The chamber is rectangular, built of three uprights; the capstone is not preserved.

11: Tillitse: 10 km south of Nakskov. Outside the porch of the parish church is a rune-stone with two inscriptions. On the broader side of the stone is written, 'Eskil Sulkesøn erected this stone to himself. While the stone lives this inscription will stay forever which Eskil carved. Christ and St. Michael help his soul'. On the narrow side of the stone is the inscription, 'Toke carved the runes to his stepmother Thora, a well-bred woman'.

12: Tågerup: 5 km south-east of Rødby. On the outer wall of the porch of Tågerup parish church is a rune-stone with the following inscription, 'Østen's sons erected this stone to their brother Spærle, Esbern Næb's skipper'.

The principal museum of Lolland—and of Falster (Area 20) as well—is Lolland–Falsters Stiftsmuseum at Maribo (Jernbanegade) with good collections especially of Mesolithic settlement sites, and finds from the many megalithic tombs. The museum is open from 10–12 noon and 2–6 p.m. (from March to November) and from 2–4 p.m. (November–February).

Maribo, the county town of Lolland and Falster, is well suited for visits to the sites Nos. 1 and 7. Several coach routes and train connections to Nykøbing and Nakskov. The Tourist Information Office is at Jernbanegade 8. Hotels: Hvide Hus; Dana, Suhrsgade 13; Ebsen's Hotel, Vestergade 32.

Nakskov is a good starting point for visits to the sites Nos. 6 and 11. The coach station is at the railway station. Train connections to

Nykøbing–Maribo and Kragenæs. Ferry to Langeland. Hotels: Harmonien, Nybrogade 2; Skandinavien, Vejlegade 33; Børsen, Østergade 12; Missionshotellet, Havnegade 21.

Sakskøbing is well situated for visits to the sites Nos. 2, 4, 5, 9 and 10. The coach station is at the railway station. Train connections to Nykøbing–Nakskov. The Tourist Information Office is at Thaaning Steffensens bookshop. Hotels: Hotel Sakskøbing, Torvet.

Rødby is well situated for a visit to site No. 12. The coach station is at Østergade 36. Train connections Copenhagen–Rødby Ferry (to Germany). Hotels: Danhotel, Rødbyhavn (5 km from Rødby); Motel Rødbyhavn. In Rødby town: Eggert's Hotel and Landmandshotellet, Vestergade 6.

Nysted is well situated for visits to sites Nos. 3 and 8 (site No. 8 is just as easily approached from Nykøbing Falster, see Area 20). Hotels: Nysted Hotel, Adelgade 35; Bogtrykkeriets Motel, Adelgade 16.

Area 20. Falster

1: Fiskebæk Skov: 16 km south of Nykøbing by A2. West of the road is the small wood, Fiskebæk Skov, just south of Gedsergård Manor. In the centre of the wood are some enigmatic rows of stones from 50 to 80 m long, and seemingly put up in pairs with a distance of 4–6 m between the rows and about double this distance between the pairs. They may be connected with the three long dolmens in the immediate vicinity. In the southern part of the wood is a small passage grave, the oval chamber is 3 m long, the uncovered passage measures 5 m. About 100 m west of the chamber are three small, low barrows from the Late Bronze Age.

2: Halskov Vænge is a tiny little wood (about 1 km square) 15 km east of Nykøbing by the road through Sdr Kirkeby and Karleby to Halskov, the wood is between Halskov and Skjoltrup villages. In the western part of the wood is a group of small barrows and an enormous stone with two cup-marks. In the southern part is a group of about twenty small barrows placed very close together; most of them are surrounded by peristaliths and bauta stones are placed near them. Near this group is a fine long dolmen with twenty-seven large peristaliths; 100 m further north is another long dolmen the chamber of which is covered by a gigantic capstone. Just outside the south-eastern corner of the wood is a dolmen chamber, all that is left of a round dolmen.

3: Korselitze Østerskov: North-east of Halskov Vænge by Brejninge and Bønnet to Hesnæs. Just north of Hesnæs and the forester's house is Ørnehøj (i.e. Eagle's hill), a long dolmen, 30 m long with about forty peristaliths still in place (on one is carved F.C.C. 1843: i.e. Frederik VII, who excavated the chamber in 1843). In the centre of the mound is a passage grave without capstones; the chamber is 8 m long. West of Ørnehøj is a group of twenty-nine barrows from the Late Bronze Age; more groups of such small barrows can be found also in the northern part of the wood.

The Falster sites are all within easy reach of Nykøbing, the largest
town of the island. The coach station is at the Railway Station Square.
Train connections to Copenhagen–Gedser/Rødby and to Nakskov. The
Tourist Information Office is at the Railway Station Square. Hotels:
Baltic, Jernbanegade 47; Phoenix, Jernbanegade 19; Industrihotellet,
Torvet 3; Missionshotellet, Tværgade 3; Motel Liselund, Sundby
(2 km from the town).

Area 21. Møn

1: Bogø: is a small island in the sound Storstrømmen between Zealand, Falster and Møn. Bogø is reached either from Falster by ferry from Stubbekøbing, or from Møn by the bridge west of Fanefjord. This tiny island (about 5 × 3 km) is very rich in megalithic monuments. In the wood Østerskov are five long dolmens near the coast and in the north-western part is the passage grave Hulehøj; the chamber is 6.5 m long and the passage has a length of 6 m. About 1 km north of Bogø church is Ellenæs Hage where stands a long dolmen, 25 m long, with two chambers both of which have a short passage. Near the coast north of Vestenskov is a long dolmen, 28 m long, with two rectangular chambers. It is most unusual that both chambers are placed parallel to the sides of the dolmen instead of at right angles.

2: Busene: In the south-eastern part of Møn south of the wood Klinteskoven is a tiny patch of wood called Busene Have, in which is a pretty group of eight Bronze Age barrows, a bauta stone, and a square enclosure made of seventeen stones.

3: Grønjægers Høj: 13 km south-west of Stege and about 0.5 km south of Fanefjord parish church is one of the finest and most impressive Danish long dolmens. The mound is 102 m long and 10 m broad. 134 peristaliths frame the mound which has three chambers. Only one chamber has the capstone preserved.

4: Jordehøj: 3 km south-west of Stege on the road to Damshølte and just north of the road is the passage grave Jordehøj. The chamber is 10 × 25 m, built of twenty-four uprights and six capstones, the passage is 8 m long. The chamber was opened in 1836 and the old report says that '6–8 big bodies lay in rows, many stone implements, also some of bone and in the corners stood clay vessels'. The finds are in the National Museum. 3 km further south, about 0.5 km east of Æbelnæs village, is a very fine passage grave, the chamber is 10 m long and the passage

Plate 15. The chamber of the passage grave, 'Kong Askers høj' in the island of Møn (Area 21, No. 6)

7 m. The chamber has the same peculiarity as Jordehøj in that it is broader at the ends—this feature is characteristic of the passage graves in Møn.

5: Klekkendehøj: 12 km west of Stege, turn at the 10 km stone and go by the road to Røddinge village. The passage grave Klekkendehøj is just south of the road. The mound covers the only double passage grave in Møn. The 9 m long chamber is divided into two by a transverse wall of stones, each part having its own passage of about 8 m length. The chamber was excavated in the 1790's by the owner of the land who bequeathed the finds to the newly founded National Museum in 1807.

6: Kong Askers Høj: About 12 km west of Stege and 1 km west of Sprove village. This passage grave is one of the largest and most beautiful in the country. The chamber is 10 m long and 2 m broad, it is built of nineteen uprights and six capstones. The passage is built of nine pairs of uprights and six capstones, the length is 10 m.

7: Marienborg: 7 km west of Stege by the road to Damsholte is Marienborg Manor; just north of the park is a faked long dolmen, built about 1800 when romantic notions of the past and landscape gardening were alike fashionable. The stones are, sadly enough, taken from real dolmens in the immediate vicinity of the Manor.

8: The Sømarke dolmen: 15 km east of Stege and just beside the road from Sømarke to Liselund Manor is a large dolmen chamber built of six uprights and one capstone. The small passage is built of three uprights and one capstone which is covered with cup-marks.

Møns Museum, near the 'Mølleport' at Stege, has a small archaeological collection of local finds. The museum is open daily in the summer season from 10–12 noon and 2–4 p.m., Wednesdays also from 7–9 p.m. It is closed from November to May.

Stege is the capital of Møn, a pretty little town with many old houses and a beautiful church. The coach station is at Storegade 78, the Tourist Information Office at Langgade 1. Hotels: Harmonien, Storegade 12; Bjerrehus, Storegade 10.

Area 22. Bornholm

Bornholm—the pretty rock island in the Baltic Sea—is reached by ship from Copenhagen (departure every evening from Havnegade) or by air (several daily connections) from Kastrup Airport.

1: Arnager: 8 km south-east of Rønne. A small passage grave which was excavated by the National Museum in 1938. The finds were two clay urns, two flint blades, about twenty-five amber beads and also traces of about fifteen human skulls.

2: Bjælkestenen: Rune-stone placed just south of Åkirkeby by the road to Pedersker. Only a fragment of the stone is preserved, the inscription on which reads, 'Thorsten, a well-bred Thegn had (the stone) carved to Sven (?)'.

3: Blemmelyng: About 8 km east of Rønne by the road to Østerlars. Turn south at the 5 km stone. Between the road and Blemmegård farm are several prehistoric fields to be seen. The enclosures date from the Late Bronze Age or the Early Iron Age.

4: The Brogård rune-stone is placed at the crossroads 2 km south-east of Hasle. The inscription reads, 'Svenger erected this stone to his father Toste and to his brother Alvlak and to his mother and his sister'.

5: The Brohus rune-stone: 11 km north-west of Neksø just by the road to Østermarie. The stone was once used as building material and broken to pieces, it is now repaired with strips of iron bands. The inscription reads, 'Bove had the stone carved to Thykil'.

6: Bøgebjerg: 8 km south of Gudhjem by the road to Østerlarsker, then south by the road which leads to the Rønne–Svaneke road. 1.5 km south of Østerlarsker, and west of the road is Bøgebjerg past a stretch of meadow on a sloping hillside. First there are two bauta stones and further east is a group of stone cists dating from the Viking period, excavated in 1879 and restored in 1954–6. Placed centrally on the hillside is a mound which covered a burial from the Late Roman Iron Age.

7: Bøsthøj: 5 km south of Åkirkeby and 1 km north of the Rønne–Pedersker road. An imposing mound at the foot of which can be seen three stone cists which contained burials from the Early Bronze Age.

8: Enesbjerg and Galgebakken (the Gallows hill): 10 km east of Rønne in the immediate vicinity of Vestermarie are three cairns and a ship-formed burial, and 0.5 km south-east of these monuments a protected area with seventeen cairns and two ship-formed burials. The date is uncertain but it may be late Bronze Age or Earliest Iron Age.

9: Falhøj: 13 km south-west of Neksø by the road to Rønne, turn south by the road to Ø. Sømarkshuse. Along this road are several Bronze Age barrows among which Alhøj and Falhøj are the largest and best preserved.

10: Gamleborg, Almindingen: A hill-fort placed on top of a rock plateau and protected by a wall which is up to 6 m high. The refuge dates from the Viking period and the Middle Ages. In the latter period the walls were reinforced in parts with hewn limestones which are known also from the round churches.

11: Gamleborg, Paradisbakkerne: 5 km north-west of Neksø by the road through Klinteby. A hill-fort dating from the Migration period (about A.D. 500) and the Viking Age, built on a 14 m high rock plateau and protected by a wall of earth and stones where the slope was not considered steep enough. The refuge was excavated by the National Museum in 1949–51.

12: Gryet: is a tiny patch of wood 5 km west of Neksø (turn north at Bodilsker church). In the wood are fifty-six bauta stones from the Viking period.

13: Gudhjem: On the steep rocks facing the sea are two bauta stones called 'Hestestenene' (i.e. The Horse's Stones). Just south of the road which passes south of the town is a protected area with twenty cairns

9

Plate 16. One of the ships from the rock engravings at Storlykkebakken, Hammeren, Bornholm (Area 22, No. 14)

and four bauta stones. About 0.5 km west of the town on the beach is a protected area with rectangular stone enclosures and several cairns. (It is strictly forbidden to remove stones from the cairns.)

14: Hammeren: The north-western point of Bornholm is rich in fine rock engravings. The farm **Brogård** is on the road Hasle–Allinge, about 1.5 km from Allinge (a road sign indicates the rock engravings), the engraving depicts five ships with high bows. **Madsebakke** is halfway between Allinge and Sandvig (follow the road sign on the coast road), the richest group of rock engravings to be found in Denmark: twelve ships, a wheel with four spokes surrounded by and filled with cup-marks, several foot-prints, and many cup-marks. **Storlykke-bakken** is 1 km south of Allinge on the road to Olsker; the rock is decorated with three ships, foot-prints, and cup-marks.

15: 'Helligkvinde' (i.e. 'The Sacred Woman'): is the name of the two bauta stones which stand by the coast road to Gudhjem, 3 km west of Svaneke. The larger of the two, 'The Sacred Woman', stands on a ruined cairn. The oval stone enclosure nearby is called 'The Sacred Woman's Children'. Until quite recently all wayfarers made their bow to 'The Sacred Woman'.

16: Hjortebakkerne: About 6 km west of Neksø, just south of the road (to Åkirkeby), is a pretty group of bauta stones some of which form a circle. The date is uncertain but may be the Viking period.

17: Jættedal: 4 km south of Åkirkeby (turn south at Hundshale to Krusegård) is a passage grave which was excavated in 1883; the rich finds from the Middle Neolithic period number many amber beads, flint arrow-heads, slate pendants and sherds of several vessels.

18: Lundestenen: 10 km south-east of Rønne by the coast road leading to Pedersker, turn north at the 10 km stone; 1.5 km north of the 10 km stone and west of the road is a passage grave which was excavated by the National Museum in 1939. The finds comprise many amber beads and pendants, flint arrow-heads, and two clay vessels.

19: Louisenlund: 5 km west of Svaneke by the Rønne road. Near the 25 km stone, south of the road is a small wood with fifty bauta stones surrounded by a stone fence. Burials connected with the stones seem not to have existed, but the area has never been excavated; it dates probably from the Viking period.

20: Rispebjerg: 10 km south-west of Neksø by the road through Poulsker; about 1.5 km west of Poulsker turn north through the wood where a lane leads to the hill-fort 'Ringborgen' dating from the Late Iron Age. To the north and west are steep rocks, to the south and east the place is protected by a ditch and a wall up to 3 m high and 115 m long; the entrances face west and east. Rispebjerg was also inhabited during the Middle Neolithic period but most of the culture layer is now found in the walls which were built during the Late Iron Age. About 400 m to the east is another wall, 'Bukkediget', 2 m high which may have served as an extra protection for Rispebjerg.

21: Sellehøj: 2 km north-west of Neksø near the farm Rågeskovgård is a passage grave, Sellehøj, which was excavated in 1890 (the chamber) and in 1919 (the passage and the area outside the passage). In the chamber were found several skulls, some amber beads, and a few potsherds. Outside the passage were found sherds of about 200 vessels, most of them richly decorated. The finds date from the Middle Neolithic period.

22: Stammershalle: Halfway between Gudhjem and Allinge, between the road and the sea is a protected area with Iron Age burials: two stone cists framed by stone enclosures dating from the Roman Iron Age, a bauta stone in the centre of a star-shaped stone frame which covered a cremation patch of Roman Iron Age date, several small bauta stones covering cremation patches, and a cairn in which was once found an Early Bronze Age inhumation grave.

23: Stensebygård: 5 km south-west of Neksø about 0.5 km from Bodilsker station is a passage grave without capstones. The chamber was excavated in 1892; it contained several amber beads and an ornamented clay vessel; a later excavation (1923) outside the entrance brought to light about 3,000 potsherds dating from the Middle Neolithic period. 200 m to the south is another passage grave which has—most unusually—capstones made of sandstone instead of granite. The chamber was excavated in 1882 and was found to contain more than 200 amber beads and pendants, a few potsherds, and a slate knife.

24: Svaneke: offers the archaeologically-minded traveller many sights worth seeing: **Frennegård** is about 1 km south of the town halfway between the coast road and the road to Ibsker, here are two granite rocks with cup-marks. Round the southern one is a stone circle and near it a bauta stone. At **Frennemark,** 1 km to the east just beside the coast road, stand three fine bauta stones. **Grisby,** 0.5 km south of the bauta stones of Frennemark, has five bauta stones standing on gravel pillars —as gravel digging has removed a thick layer of the surface soil. **Hallebrøndshøj** is a passage grave halfway between Svaneke and Ibsker, east of the road. The chamber was excavated in 1884; the finds, which are in Bornholms Museum, comprise about 200 amber beads, four flint axes, two clay vessels, and a slate pendant. **Listed,** 1.5 km north-west of Svaneke, two bauta stones stand between the road and the coast. **Ormehøj,** 3 km south of Svaneke and just north of Skovsholm farm, has three stone cists of which one dates from the Early Bronze Age. During the excavation in 1908 it was found to contain an inhumation grave with a bronze dagger, a small axe, and a 'strike-a-light' of flint.

25: Tillehøje: 5 km north of Rønne, not far from the road in the Blykobbe plantation, is a group of Bronze Age barrows. One of the mounds was excavated in 1824 by Crown Prince Christian (later Christian VIII), who found a Bronze Age burial.

26: Varperne: 10 km north-west of Neksø by the road to Åkirkeby. Turn north along the road leading to Pedersker plantation (the road goes on to Ølene); just beside the road are three cairns, between two of them an ancient trackway can be seen. The cairns are still decorated with flowers and greenery as the story goes that three sisters who were killed by their brothers lie buried here.

27: Vasegård: About 2 km south-west of Åkirkeby and beside the river Læsåen is a long barrow at the eastern end of which is a pentagonal dolmen chamber covered by a large capstone; in this chamber was found a secondary burial of Bronze Age date. In the western end of the barrow is a rectangular stone cist dating from the Bronze Age.

28: Ørnekullerne: 1 km south of Hasle in the northern part of the wood is a group of eight excavated cairns which were examined in 1833 and found to contain Iron Age cremation patches. This is the first scientific excavation known in Bornholm and the finds were of great importance to C. J. Thomsen when he was working out his famous 'Three period system'. They also convinced him of the existence of a 'pre-Christian Iron Age'.

The principal museum is Bornholms Museum, Sct Mortensgade 29, Rønne, which possesses excellent collections of the prehistory of the island. The museum is open during the summer season (1st May–31st October) from 2–5 p.m., Sundays from 1–4 p.m., from 1st June–31st August also open daily from 10–12 noon and from 2–5 p.m. During the winter season open on Sundays, Tuesdays and Thursdays from 1–4 p.m.

Rønne is a good starting point for visits to the sites Nos. 1, 3, 4, 8, 18 and 25. The coach station is at the railway station. The Tourist Information Office is at Jernbanevej. Hotels: Dam's hotel, Krystalgade 11; Bornholm, Borgergade 19; Hotel Dana, Østergade 54; Fredensborg, Strandvejen; Rønne Missionshotel, Grønnegade 17–19.

Hasle is well situated for visits to the sites 4, 14 and 28 (Hasle is only 11 km north of Rønne). The coach station is at Krummevej 2. The Tourist Information Office is at the bookseller's, Storegade 60. Hotels: Herold, Vestergade 65; Vendelbogård, Grønnegade 3.

Neksø is good for visits to the sites Nos. 5, 9, 11, 12, 16, 20, 21, 23 and 26. The coach station is at the railway station. The Tourist Information Office is at Torvegade 2. Hotels: Centralhotellet; Holm's hotel, Torvegade 5; Hotel Neksø.

Åkirkeby is well suited for visits to the sites Nos. 2, 7, 10, 17 and 27. The coach station is at the railway station. The Tourist Information Office is at the bookseller's, Eskildsgade 3. Hotels: Kann's hotel, Eskildsgade 6; Højskolehotellet, Østergade 9.

Svaneke should be the starting point for visits to the sites Nos. 15, 19 and 24. The Tourist Information Office is at Postgade 15. Hotels: Siemsen's gård, Havnegade 9; Josephsen's hotel, Storegade; Østersøen, Havnegade.

Gudhjem is well situated for visits to the sites Nos. 6, 13 and 23. The Tourist Information Office is at the harbour. Hotels: Afholdshotellet (not licensed), Brøddegade; Jantzen's hotel, Brøddegade; Fuglsang, Havnepladsen; Thern's hotel, Brøddegade.

Bibliography

Very few popular works on Danish prehistory have been published in international languages:

Johs. Brøndsted, *Nordische Vorzeit I–III*. Neumünster 1960–3.

Johs. Brøndsted, *The Vikings*, Penguin Books, 1960.

P. V. Glob, *Mosefolket* (English translation, *The Bog People*, published by Faber and Faber, London, and Cornell University Press, in 1969).

O. Klindt-Jensen, *Denmark before the Vikings*. (Ancient Peoples and Places Series). London 1957.

Palle Lauring, *Land of the Tollund Man*, London 1958.

Palle Lauring, *A History of Denmark*, (p. 1–61), London 1964.

Holger Rasmussen, *Prehistoric Dane*, Copenhagen 1956.

P. H. Sawyer, *The Age of the Vikings*, Edward Arnold, London 1962.

Several small pamphlets published by the Danish National Museum deal with the more important prehistoric sites. The following have been translated into English:

Poul Nørlund, *Trelleborg*.

Olaf Olsen, *Fyrkat*.

Knud Thorvildsen, *The Ladby Ship Burial*.

The Danish periodicals *Kuml* (Aarhus 1951 ff.), *Aarbøger for nordisk Oldkyndighed og Historie* (Copenhagen 1866 ff.), and *Acta archaeologica* (Copenhagen 1931 ff.) deal with any subject of Danish prehistory. *Acta arch.* is written in English, French and German, the other periodicals have English or German summaries.

Index